MEET
THE
NEXT
PRESIDENT

WHAT YOU DON'T KNOW ABOUT
THE CANDIDATES

BILL SAMMON

THRESHOLD
EDITIONS

NEW YORK LONDON TORONTO SYDNEY

Threshold Editions
A Division of Simon & Schuster, Inc.
1230 Avenue of the Americas
New York, NY 10020

First Threshold Editions hardcover edition December 2007

THRESHOLD EDITIONS and colophon are trademarks of Simon & Schuster, Inc.

For information about special discounts for bulk purchases, please contact Simon & Schuster Special Sales at 1-800-456-6798 or business@simonandschuster.com.

Designed by Ruth Lee-Mui

Manufactured in the United States of America

10   9   8   7   6   5   4   3   2   1

ISBN 978-1-4516-6899-5

To Blair

CONTENTS

FOREWORD

Barack Obama once came close to injecting heroin, but balked when a junkie pulled out the needle and rubber tubing. Obama and Mitt Romney are descended from polygamous great-grandfathers who had five wives apiece. Rudy Giuliani's first wife was his second cousin. Liberal Democrat Hillary Rodham Clinton was once a conservative Republican "Goldwater Girl."

Such are the plot twists in the remarkable saga of the 2008 presidential campaign, which is brimming with enough colorful characters to populate a Russian novel. On second thought, no novelist would dare invent such an audacious cast of characters in a single work of fiction. After all, who could be expected to believe in the existence of Fred Thompson, an actor who has grown tired of playing presidents on TV? Or John Edwards, a populist who pays four hundred dollars for a haircut? Or John McCain, an aging war hero who can't stop alienating his own party?

Even the subplots wouldn't pass the laugh test. Surely there

could not be someone named Bill Richardson, who was actually raised in Mexico and once summoned Monica Lewinsky to
his Watergate apartment for a job interview. And no self-
respecting purveyor of believable fiction would ever dream up
Mike Huckabee, who once strode into an important meeting
and authoritatively planted himself in a chair that collapsed
under his own staggering weight.

And yet one of these all-too-human mortals will soon become the most powerful person on the planet. Journalists who
have been tasked with chronicling the election are thanking
their lucky stars for this bonanza of irresistible personalities.
They are also grateful for the historic nature of this election.
For the first time in more than half a century, the field of White
House hopefuls does not include an incumbent president or
vice president. That means 2008 is a wide-open race on both
sides of the political aisle. In the past, presidential elections have
often been lopsided affairs, generating about as much excite-
ment as a Super Bowl blowout. But the 2008 race has all the
makings of a nail-biter, with every vote counting down the
home stretch.

All of which makes it absolutely imperative for voters to fa-
miliarize themselves with the field. Who are these candidates?
What do they stand for? How are they running their campaigns? Only when these questions are answered can Americans intelligently ponder an even more important set of
queries.

Who can be trusted to prosecute the next phase of the war
on terror? Who should tell the nation whether taxes will rise
or fall? Who deserves the awesome power to appoint the next

Supreme Court justices, whose momentous decisions will affect Americans for generations? Who can best guide the world's sole superpower into the second decade of the twenty-first century, when rogue regimes could alter the global balance of power with nuclear weapons?

In short, who will be the forty-fourth president of the United States?

MEET
THE
NEXT
PRESIDENT

MITT ROMNEY

O f all the people seeking the White House in 2008, none actually *look* as presidential as Mitt Romney. Tall, lantern-jawed, and blessed with a shock of raven hair (flecked gray at the temples, of course), the former Massachusetts governor seems to have been plucked directly from central casting for a starring role at 1600 Pennsylvania Avenue. The presidential aura grows only stronger when he opens his mouth to speak. Upbeat, articulate, quick-witted, and self-deprecating, the rich Republican seems more like a movie-star president than even Fred Thompson, an actual movie star president who, in an odd twist, is now vying with Romney for the real-life presidency.

Even on paper, Romney has adopted precisely the correct positions to appeal to the conservative activists whose support he considers crucial. He is more conservative than John Mc-Cain on taxes, Rudy Giuliani on gay marriage, Mike Huckabee on immigration, and Fred Thompson on campaign finance. Like most other top GOP contenders, Romney supports the vigorous prosecution of the war on terror, including the establishment of a democracy in Iraq. And perhaps most important, from a conservative perspective, Romney calls himself staunchly pro-life.

There's just one problem. Romney used to be staunchly pro-choice. Critics say he cravenly flip-flopped in order to have a shot at the presidency. But Romney insists he underwent a genuine change of heart on abortion while grappling with a related issue, stem cell research, in 2004. His ability to convince conservatives of the sincerity of that conversion will go a long way toward determining his electoral success.

But there is an even larger obstacle that could keep Romney from clinching the White House—his religion. Mitt Romney belongs to the Mormon Church, which is considered a cult by many evangelical Christians, who are an influential voting bloc. Romney must assure these skeptical evangelicals, and ultimately all of America, that his faith does not disqualify him from holding the highest office in the land.

A HISTORY OF BELIEVERS

It is impossible to trace Mitt Romney's ancestry without also tracing the origin of the Mormon Church. Romney's great-great-grandfather, English architect Miles Archibald Romney, converted to Mormonism in 1837, just seven years after the church was founded in America by Joseph Smith, Jr. According to Mitt, Miles "was convinced by Mormon missionaries that the church of God had been restored to the earth by a young prophet in New York State." So, in 1841, Miles left his established practice in Dalton-in-Furness, a village 220 miles northwest of London, and sailed to America. As Mitt recounted in his 2004 memoir, *Turnaround,* Miles "joined with the 'saints' in Nauvoo, Illinois," a tiny town on the Mississippi River where Smith was establishing his fledgling church. Three years later, Smith was assassinated and his followers fled to Utah.

Miles had a son, Miles Park Romney, who grew up to marry Hannah Hood Hill, Mitt's great-grandmother, in 1862. Although polygamy was outlawed by President Lincoln two months after the wedding, the younger Miles ended up taking multiple wives. His defiance of U.S. law was urged by Brigham Young, who succeeded Smith as president of the Mormon Church. As an outlaw polygamist, Miles Park Romney was forced in 1885 to flee to Mexico, where he married his fifth wife. By then he was the father of at least seventeen children, including a fourteen-year-old boy named Gaskell, Mitt's grandfather, who had been born in Utah.

In 1895, while living in Mexico, Gaskell married fellow Utah native Anna Amelia Pratt. The wedding came five years after the Mormon Church reversed itself on polygamy by issuing a ban that continues to this day. Accordingly, Gaskell remained monogamous. He and his wife had seven children, including George, Mitt's father, who was born in 1907 in Chihuahua, Mexico. Five years later, as the Mexican Revolution plunged the nation into turmoil, the Romneys fled to the United States, eventually settling in Salt Lake City.

In 1931, George married his high-school sweetheart, Lenore LaFount, and within a decade the couple had two daughters, Lynn and Jane, as well as a son, Scott. Although Lenore was subsequently told by her doctor that a medical condition would prohibit further childbearing, she had another boy, Willard Mitt Romney, on March 12, 1947, nearly six years after Scott. The child was named after fellow Mormon J. Willard Marriott, a family friend who would go on to start a chain of hotels, and Milton "Mitt" Romney, George's cousin who had played quarterback for the Chicago Bears in the 1920s. George and Lenore doted on young Mitt, whom they considered their "miracle baby."

"He was a great dad, and Mom was an extraordinary mom," Mitt Romney told me. "I mean, my mom read to me, as a little boy, she read from *Idylls of the King* by Tennyson. And we'd read that nightly. I think one of the reasons I became an English major was that my mom was so steeped in literature and English and I loved to write and loved to read, by virtue of that home education."

While young Mitt idolized his father, he acquired his love of practical jokes from his mother.

"My mom had a great sense of humor. My dad's sense of humor was severely lacking," Romney told me, chuckling at the memory. "He was incapable of telling a joke. And when the rest of the family was laughing, he'd get mad and tell us to stop laughing. I love laughing."

After moving from Detroit to the affluent suburb of Bloom-field Hills, George became chairman and CEO of the struggling American Motors Corporation (AMC) in 1954. Deriding large cars as "gas-guzzling dinosaurs," George staked the company's future on the Rambler, a compact car. Sales sky-rocketed, AMC flourished, and George was hailed as a turn-around artist, even making the cover of *Time* magazine. Young Mitt was mesmerized.

"I saw my father grab the reins of a failing car company," he recalled. "It was one of the most powerful experiences of my childhood watching him turn American Motors around."

By the early 1960s, George was dabbling in politics. He even found a way to involve his beloved son Mitt, who was enrolled at Cranbrook, an elite college preparatory school for boys in Bloomfield Hills.

"As a fourteen-year-old, I went up with my dad collecting signatures for something called Citizens for Michigan, which called for a new constitution for Michigan," Mitt told me. "And he would pull up in a softball field and give me the clipboard and say, 'Go get as many signatures as you can.' He'd sit in the car. And I wondered why he was sending me out for the signa-tures, but now I recognize it was the age-old ploy of teaching by getting your child to do. And I learned how to go out in the crowds and to gather signatures and to explain why a new con-stitution was needed in Michigan."

Warming to politics, George entered the Michigan guber-natorial race as a Republican in 1962. As usual, he took Mitt along for the ride.

"When he ran for governor the first time, I was fifteen,"

Mitt told me. "I went in a microbus, these little, we now call them minivans, but we drove all over Michigan, ultimately to all eighty-three of Michigan's counties. I'd go to the county fair, we'd set up a booth, I'd hand out brochures. Had a microphone and little speakers on top of the truck and we'd talk with people about why George Romney would be good for Michigan. So I know the state corner to corner, I've visited every county, and it's an extraordinarily beautiful and warm place."

George won the election and went on to serve three terms. Meanwhile, Mitt had fallen for a girl, Ann Davies, who attended Kingswood School, the all-girls counterpart to Cranbrook. Ann was just fifteen and Mitt was eighteen when they met at the birthday party of a mutual friend. For their first date, Mitt took Ann to the film *The Sound of Music*. Before long, Mitt was "completely, totally hooked" on Ann, he told me.

"I was fully in love with her, asked her if she'd marry me, she said she would, and we started making plans," he said.

But those plans entailed years of separation before any wedding could take place. In 1965, Mitt graduated from Cranbrook and headed to California to attend Stanford University. A year later, he interrupted his college career and moved to France to proselytize for his church. He got a lot of doors slammed in his face as he tried to convert the French to Mormonism.

"That was a very formative experience for me," Romney told me.

Having grown up in a world of privilege, he now found himself surviving on a shoestring budget.

"I lived very modestly in France," he told me. "At that time, I drew down one hundred dollars a month for everything—

health, housing, clothing, food, transportation. And I know it was a long time ago, but one hundred dollars was still not very much money. I lived in apartments that in some cases didn't have toilets. We had an in-house outhouse, if you will, a hole in the floor. You stepped on the footpads and pulled the chain for the bucket of water to empty it.

"When I lived in Paris, we were in an apartment that shared the toilet facility with three or four other apartments on our floor," he added. "We did have a toilet in Bordeaux, but we shared with the other apartment across the way. We showered in public showers. And that's not unusual for people in France. But it was unusual for a guy who'd grown up in the home of an automobile executive to live so modestly."

Back in the States, Mitt's father decided to run for the Republican presidential nomination. Although he had been born in Mexico, his parents had never relinquished their U.S. citizenship, which allowed George to meet the Constitution's "natural born citizen" requirement for the presidency.

George's campaign got off to a strong start, but he committed a major gaffe in August 1967 that would ultimately doom his campaign. He remarked to a Detroit broadcaster that he had turned against the Vietnam War after being subjected to a "brainwashing." The comment triggered widespread criticism, forcing George to pull out of the race in February 1968. His consolation prize was to be appointed secretary of housing and urban development by the victorious President Nixon.

A few months later, twenty-one-year-old Mitt was involved in a horrific car crash in France. A Mercedes driven by a Catholic priest crossed the center line and slammed head-on into the Citroën driven by Mitt. The impact killed a woman in Mitt's car.

"I was also pronounced dead," he recalled in *Turnaround*. "One of the gendarmes at the scene found me lying unconscious on the side and wrote '*Il est mort*' on my passport before moving on. The erroneous accident report was picked up by a news service that broadcast the report in the United States. My parents and Ann, my then-girlfriend and future wife, learned that I had expired."

Refusing to believe the news, Mitt's father, George, called a friend in Paris, Sargent Shriver, the U.S. ambassador to France, who was able to ascertain that his son had indeed survived. Although Mitt was hospitalized with a broken arm and bruised forehead, he made a full recovery. He even began to take a more active role in the mission.

TURNAROUND ARTIST

In December 1968, Mitt returned to the States and renewed his offer of marriage to Ann, who again accepted. The wedding took place in March 1969. After exchanging vows in a civil ceremony in Michigan, the bride and groom flew to Salt Lake City and were married again, or "sealed," in the Mormon temple. Ann had converted to Mormonism while Mitt was in France, but her parents, as non-Mormons, were not allowed inside the temple.

Mitt stayed in Utah, having transferred from Stanford to Brigham Young University, the Mormon college, to resume his undergraduate studies as an English major. In 1970, Ann gave birth to their first son. That same year, Mitt's mother, Lenore, ran unsuccessfully for the U.S. Senate from Michigan.

In 1971, after graduating from Brigham Young, Romney moved to Boston to attend graduate school at Harvard, from which he emerged in 1975 with degrees in law and business administration. By now the father of three young sons, he quickly turned to making his fortune.

Romney was recruited by Boston Consulting Group (BCG) and worked there two years before moving to Bain & Company, a rival consulting firm founded by a BCG alumnus, Bill Bain. The new company specialized in turning around troubled enterprises. Romney and other consultants would begin each turnaround with a "strategic audit," which entailed immersing themselves in reams of data and analyzing it in ways the clients had not previously considered. Reforms were then implemented, usually restoring the companies to profitability.

Romney, now the father of five sons, was persuaded by Bill Bain to expand the Bain empire in 1983 by launching a venture capital start-up. The sister firm was dubbed Bain Capital and began investing heavily in promising young enterprises, such as Staples office supplies and Domino's pizza. When these ventures became runaway successes, Romney and his partners grew enormously wealthy. It was obvious that Romney's skills as a consultant carried over into the world of venture capital.

"My responsibilities were as a leader, but also as an analytical thinker," he told me. "My job entailed gathering data, interpreting it, analyzing it and finding creative solutions to problems, both as an investor and as a consultant."

Although Bain Capital was flourishing under Romney's

leadership, the original Bain & Company eventually fell on hard times. In 1990, Bill Bain persuaded Romney to leave Bain Capital in order to lead a turnaround of the mothership. Romney succeeded and then returned to Bain Capital in 1991. He would not stay long.

"In 1993, something almost irrational happened," he wrote in *Turnaround*. "I began thinking about making a run against Senator Ted Kennedy."

Romney indeed mounted a run and came closer than any other Republican to unseating the liberal icon in 1994.

"For a moment, just after I won the primary election, I was even tied or slightly ahead in the polls. But then Kennedy came back strong," Romney wrote in *Turnaround*. "His ads reinforced people's misperceptions about me as money-grubbing businessman. He injected my Mormonism into the campaign in a highly visible way. Our polls showed that my faith was a significant negative in largely Catholic Massachusetts."

Mindful that Massachusetts was also largely pro-choice, Romney broke with the Republican Party over the issue of abortion.

"I believe that abortion should be safe and legal in this country," Romney said in a 1994 debate. "I have since the time when my mom took that position when she ran in 1970 as a U.S. Senate candidate."

But his pro-choice stance was not enough to close the gap. In the end, Romney garnered just 41 percent of the vote, or seventeen points short of Kennedy's 58 percent. Still, it was the narrowest margin of victory for Kennedy in nine Senate contests.

Stung by defeat, Romney returned to Bain Capital, which

"was paying ever more spectacular dividends," he recalled in *Turnaround*. He described his work as "extraordinarily lucrative." Indeed, he continued to amass significant personal wealth. He bought a summer home on Lake Winnipesaukee in New Hampshire. And he once again began to think about public service.

GOING FOR THE GOLD

The opportunity to serve arrived in 1999, when Romney was asked to rescue the scandal-plagued Winter Olympics, which were scheduled to be held in Salt Lake City in 2002. The city had landed the games after local officials lavished $1 million in gifts—including cash, Las Vegas junkets, and even college tuition payments—on delegates from the International Olympics Committee. Nervous corporations were reluctant to sponsor the games, which now faced a massive budget shortfall. It was, in short, precisely the sort of unmitigated disaster that Romney specialized in fixing.

"It was an event in deep financial distress that required turnaround," he told me.

Initially, however, Romney resisted taking the job, which would entail leaving Bain Capital.

"How could I walk away from the golden goose, especially now that it was laying even more golden eggs?" he wrote in *Turnaround*.

"We have all we need, more than we ever dreamed of having," countered his wife, Ann. "You can afford to take this job when others can't."

Besides, the job would allow Romney to return to his ances-
tral homeland of Utah, where he had built a vacation home.
His two youngest sons, Ben and Craig, would be attending
nearby Brigham Young University during the run-up to the
Olympics. (The older three boys, Tagg, Matt, and Josh, had already graduated from the school, following in the footsteps of
their father.)

So Romney accepted the position, although he declined a
salary. He spent the next three years cleaning house, putting an
end to the scandals, recruiting corporate sponsors, and pulling
off an Olympics that wowed the world just months after the
September 11 terrorist attacks.

"He managed to remove the stink of scandal and replace it
with the glow of success," the *Boston Globe* reported.

"The Olympic experience was very similar to my work
in the private sector," Romney told me. "You know, we had
tough budgets to meet, we needed to bring new sponsors into
the mix."

But it also exposed the corporate CEO to a world he had
never experienced before—government relations.

"We were highly integrated with government," he told me.
"I needed to receive support from the federal government, support from the state and local government. I had to work exten-
sively with government officials. My board members were all
appointed by either the mayor or the governor, so ultimately
my boss was the mayor and the governor. And so it . . . involved
me in the process of government far more fully."

It also involved him far more fully in foreign relations.

"Everything we did had to be approved by an international

group of leaders that I met with regularly and presented to regularly," he told me. "Therefore, the need to understand the
perspectives of foreign leaders was brought home."

Finally, the Olympics subjected Romney to a crash course in
media relations, which he said he found "very valuable."

"It is a very public event," he told me. "Most corporations
are quite private. As a matter of fact, when a corporation hears
that there's going to be an article written about them, they're
terrified. They hire a PR firm to come in and see if they can
stop the article first, and then if they can't, to try and spin it as
positively as possible. In the Olympics, we had, at the end, daily
press conferences. But even through the whole three-year period I was there, we had weekly press conferences because the
Olympics is big, international news."

Romney told me that learning "to communicate fully and
accurately to the public was a big part of that experience." He
wrote in *Turnaround* that it "taught me the importance of visi-
bility and of promptness in responding to criticism."

Having learned how to handle the media and governmental
agencies—both foreign and domestic—and having cemented
his reputation as a turnaround artist, Romney came away from
the Olympic games in 2002 with a raft of new qualifications for
the next big challenge of his life.

RED GOVERNOR, BLUE STATE

Romney parlayed these assets into a successful run for the
governorship of Massachusetts in November 2002. Upon
taking office, this results-oriented, Republican businessman

was appalled by the inefficiencies of the state's lackadaisical, overwhelmingly Democratic government.

"Romney's team inherited a fiscal meltdown," wrote the *Boston Globe*. "The incoming governor discovered the projected deficit for the following year was exploding—from $2 billion to $3 billion in a $23-billion budget."

After ordering a Bain-style "strategic audit," Romney streamlined the state's government, imposed a frugal budget, and solved the fiscal crisis without raising taxes. By 2005, Massachusetts had a surplus of $1 billion.

"Romney's success in steering the state through the fiscal maelstrom was one of his key achievements," the *Globe* reported.

Still, after a career spent mostly in the corporate world, Romney's first experience as a government official was an eye-opener.

"The private sector is far less forgiving of mistakes than the public sector," he told me. "In the public sector, if you make a mistake, well, you just raise taxes, borrow more money, and blame it on someone else.

"In the private sector, you make a mistake, you may lose your job, your company may die, you may lose the money of the banks. The consequences are very severe. There's very little forgivability of mistakes in the private sector. So the rigor of analysis and thinking that is required, the insistence on gathering data before you make conclusions and take aggressive action—that approach in the private sector is very valuable in the public sector. It just is rarely applied.

"In the public sector, typically, people come up with answers before they've even seen the data—it's based on rhetoric and polls, what they think is politically attractive. I think the public sector is far better off by having a few people, at least, who, like me, have come from a world of analysis, data, of information gathering, and problem solving."

One of the problems Romney decided to solve was the state's health care mess. Taxpayers were footing the bill for not only indigent hospital patients, but also one hundred thousand people who were making at least seventy-five thousand dollars, yet who opted against buying health care insurance.

"They could afford it," Romney told me. "They were free riders. We have a huge free rider problem in this country, which is, people say, 'Hey, I don't need to buy insurance, somebody else will pay for it.' And in my opinion the ultimate conservative approach is what we take, which is: You know what? No more ride on the government."

So Romney instituted mandatory health care insurance in Massachusetts. The state now "insists that people purchase their own insurance—private, market-based insurance," he told me.

"We didn't create a new government insurance package offered by a government agency," he explained. "There's no new government bureaucracy that creates new health care policies. Instead, we get the cost of insurance down by removing some prohibitions and mandates from our insurance laws."

Working with the conservative Heritage Foundation in Washington, Romney explained that he "found a way to allow individuals to purchase their insurance with pretax dollars. Right now, in every other state, if you want to buy the insurance yourself, rather than through your employer, you've got to pay in after-tax dollars. But we found a way to get it in pre-tax dollars."

Although the move ran counter to conservative principles of limited government, Romney was able to accomplish it without raising taxes. Furthermore, Romney told me that if elected president, he has no plans to take the Massachusetts plan national.

PRESIDENTIAL BID

Much has been written about the fact that Romney is running for president exactly forty years after his father ran for president. Indeed, the parallels between George and Mitt are striking. Both men married their high school sweethearts while in their early twenties, became governor at age fifty-five, and mounted credible campaigns for the Republican presidential nomination at age sixty. The fact that George's White House bid imploded has prompted many journalists to wonder whether Mitt is on a quest to realize his father's unfulfilled ambition. Anchorman Charlie Gibson brought it up during an interview with Romney on ABC's *Good Morning America.*

"He kept on saying, 'Well, aren't you trying to succeed where your father failed?' " Romney told me. "And I said, well that's sort of pop psychology. That is not—in any way, shape, or form—what's driving me, which is trying to, you know, fix my dad's failure. That is not what's motivating me. What's motivating me is the same sense of duty and obligation he had."

Romney certainly isn't motivated by the presidential salary of four hundred thousand dollars, which he has pledged to decline if he wins. Having amassed a quarter billion dollars in the private sector, he hasn't taken a paycheck for his public sector service since 1999, when he turned down a salary to run the Olympics. He subsequently refused a paycheck for his service as governor. Clearly, Romney did not enter the White House sweepstakes for the money. After all, if he wins, he will be the richest president in U.S. history.

So why is Mitt Romney subjecting himself and his family to the rigors of a presidential campaign that, even if he wins, will make him the target of endless political attacks and vilification? According to Romney, he's doing it because he believes he possesses the "strong leadership" that America needs at this "critical juncture."

"By virtue of circumstances, I'm one of the few who has a shot at being that person," he told me. "I see myself as being able to make a difference and therefore I have an obligation to step forward and run for office and make a personal financial contribution, give my personal time. My kids are doing the same thing."

For Romney, the stakes are too high to sit out the contest.

"In my opinion, this is one of the great inflection points in American history," he told me. "And if we take the right course here, we will remain a strong nation and the hope of the world. If we take Hillary Clinton's or Barack Obama's course, we will end up becoming a second-tier nation. It'll take decades for that to happen, but this is an inflection point in our history of great monument."

A DIM VIEW OF DEMOCRATS

Romney argues that one of his major qualifications for the presidency is his experience as a manager of corporations, the Olympics, and the Commonwealth of Massachusetts. He notes that such managerial experience is conspicuously lacking among the top Democratic presidential contenders—Hillary Clinton, Barack Obama, and John Edwards.

"None of them, so far as I know, has managed a corner store, let alone a city or a state or the government of the largest enterprise in the world," Romney told me. "They never led or managed anything. They've led their office staff."

He added: "The presidency is not an internship. You want to have someone who's actually led and managed."

Warming to his theme, Romney spells out the merits of management experience.

"The term 'management' is not terribly well understood by people at large. Leadership is generally better understood. But managing a large enterprise and getting it to change and to move and to be effective is a pretty unusual skill. Someone like Jack Welch, his success is not random. He has a set of skills which allows him to lead and manage a large enterprise like GE highly successfully, and includes a number of qualities. The ability to assess problems before they are visible to everyone else. The ability to set a vision. The ability to attract top people. The ability to lead and direct top people and give them enough rope that they can be their own manager, but at the same time giving them guidance."

In addition to lacking managerial experience, the top Democrats have a fundamentally flawed view of government and the marketplace, according to Romney. He says this view was typified by an appalling economic speech that Hillary delivered in May 2007.

"It's time for a new beginning, for an end to government of the few, by the few, and for the few," she told an audience in New Hampshire. "Time to reject the idea of an 'on your own' society and to replace it with shared responsibility for shared prosperity. I prefer a 'we're all in it together' society."

Such rhetoric is anathema to Romney, an unapologetically free-market capitalist.

"It's like, yeah, we're replacing Adam Smith with Karl Marx," he told me. "Her heartfelt view about how to make America better is a view very much akin to the view in the 1950s and sixties that Europeans had—that government really did know best. And that larger government requires larger taxes and a Big Brother mentality of, 'We know better; we can guide your life better, make you happier.' "

Romney said this same attitude was evident in Hillary's failed attempt to nationalize health care when she was the First Lady. Just as the nation rejected Hillarycare in 1994, Romney rejects Clinton's embrace of a nanny state in 2008.

"I realize it sounds like a paradox that a nation is stronger by saying to people: 'Do what's in your best interest—within the bounds of the law and morality—and that will make the nation, as a whole, better.' It's like, how can that be? Wouldn't it be smarter to have a government figuring out what's in the nation's best interest and then making everybody do that?

"The socialist method may, to some people, sound like it

makes more sense. But Adam Smith proved that was wrong. Or he posited it was wrong. And America has proved it's wrong."

Romney points to the spectacular failure of the former Soviet Union's collective economy, a central tenet of communism. He notes that the socialist economies of Europe have created virtually no new jobs in decades, while American capitalism has created tens of millions.

"And so I'm a strong believer that she is simply misguided," Romney said of Hillary. "That she, like Barack Obama and John Edwards, would take the country in a sharp left turn, making us far more like Europe, which would mean stagnation, high unemployment, inability to compete long term, a weaker military, and ultimately weaker family structure as well."

Romney also worries that Hillary, whom some regarded as the unofficial copresident when her husband was in office, would reciprocate by sharing power with Bill if she were to win the White House.

"What role would he have?" Romney said to me. "Typically the spouse is not playing an active policy role in the leadership of an administration and there's the whole question about how that would work. I think on a number of issues, it would be very confusing as to who was really in charge."

Moreover, Romney cringes at the thought of Bill Clinton's being back in the White House, once again setting a poor moral example for America's youth.

"His personal failings would be reintroduced to the culture of America, which I think would be unfortunate," he told me.

In contrast to Hillary, who began serving in the U.S. Senate in 2001, Obama did not begin his own service until 2005, making him even less qualified, according to Romney.

"I don't know that he's actually, even from a legislative standpoint, had any accomplishments of any significance," he told me.

Furthermore, Romney says Obama is utterly lacking in business acumen.

"Not having experienced the private sector at all—small business, large business—he doesn't understand how our economy actually works and therefore lives in an ivory tower type perspective of how we can be competitive," Romney told me. "Having never negotiated, having never led, you can have ideas that are fine when you're taking your first job. But when your first job of leadership and management is president of the United States, it's probably not a good place to learn on the job."

Still, Romney is not without praise for Obama.

"He's a very good speaker," he told me. "On that basis, we could say, 'Let's take this high-school graduate or college graduate, really a great speaker, and make them president, because he's just a wonderful speaker.' You'd really like them to have had some experience, to have learned from their failures and weaknesses. And I think he's missing that, Barack Obama is."

Despite these shortcomings, Romney say Obama has "a real shot" at defeating Hillary in the race for the Democratic presidential nomination.

"I would weigh that more heavily than I think the insiders are weighing it," Romney told me. "Part of that is from my experience here in Massachusetts, having watched a fellow, Deval Patrick, run for governor here with no particular political experience, as I recall, virtually no positions on important issues, but wonderful rhetoric about hope and, you know, a brighter future. And people glommed on and just loved the rhetoric."

Patrick, a black Democrat, succeeded Romney as governor in 2007. Romney believes Obama could similarly parlay his communications skills into a victory in the Democratic primaries. But regardless of whether Obama or Hillary wins the primaries, Romney is confident a Republican will prevail in the general election.

"I don't think there's any reason to think that somebody shouldn't be elected president because of their gender or their race—or their religion, for that matter," Romney told me. "I don't think Barack is the right black president. If Colin Powell were running for president, I'd feel very different.

"I don't think Hillary Clinton is the right woman to be the president of the United States. But there are a number of women who I think could very well be the next president of the United States and have the qualities of leadership that would suggest they'd be a great president. It's the *person*.

"I'm sure there are some people who won't vote for a Mormon, who won't vote for an older person, who won't vote for an ethnic minority, who won't vote for someone based on their gender. But the great majority of us don't care about those things."

As for John Edwards, Romney has a special disdain for this Democrat who made his fortune as a trial lawyer.

"I fundamentally think that the burden of excessive litigation is one of the features that makes us less competitive than we should be as a nation," Romney said. "And his fundamental belief that suing doctors and suing hospitals and suing corporations is a good thing—with massive awards—that that's a good thing, is just completely wrong and would be very harmful to the future of this country."

Although Romney was understandably disappointed by the Republican loss of Congress in 2006, he is confident that the leftward lurch by Democrats since then will ultimately backfire.

"I think they misread the '06 election," he told me. "I think they believe that the reason they got elected was because of the Democrat agenda and the liberal agenda."

Romney estimates that liberalism's appeal accounted for no more than 5 or 10 percent of the Democratic victory.

"I think what happened in '06 was people were frustrated with our conduct in the war in Iraq. And they couldn't change the coach, so they changed the team. But I don't think the nation took a sharp left and is looking for socialized medicine or for higher taxes or many of the things that the Democrats are pushing."

Romney believes Democrats are "overplaying their hand" by kowtowing to the liberal base of the Democratic Party. He is particularly critical of House Speaker Nancy Pelosi and Senate Majority Leader Harry Reid.

"I think Nancy Pelosi's highly visible visit to Syria was a huge mistake. I think Harry Reid saying we lost the war and announcing a week into the troop surge that it hasn't worked— these are, in my viewpoint, very ill-considered actions by a minority party. And think that they are violating a tradition in this country of standing united as we face a foe. We can debate amongst ourselves, but this is a mistake on their part."

Nonetheless, if elected president, Romney said he will try to restore some semblance of civility to the political debate in Washington, which he said has degenerated into "vituperative personal attacks." He is well aware that Bush failed in his own attempt to raise the level of discourse in the capital.

"I very much move in favor of civility and of restoring a working respect for people across the aisle," he told me. "You fight for that and if I fail at it, then so be it. But I'm not going to go in presuming a combative, attacking posture."

Romney emphasized that seeking common ground with Democrats does not mean abandoning Republican principles.

"There will be some places we vehemently disagree," he said. "And we should express our viewpoints and give our rhetoric with all the energy and passion that you'd expect. But there should be a level of personal respect that is between both parties—between the White House and Congress—that I think has been lacking.

"And the fact that it has failed to change over these last six years doesn't mean it's not worth trying again. Will I be more successful at it than the president? I hope so."

PARSING ABORTION

But first, in order to win the presidency, Romney will have to explain his shifting stance on abortion.

"I will preserve and protect a woman's right to choose and

am devoted and dedicated to honoring my word in that regard," Romney vowed in a gubernatorial debate in 2002. "I believe women should have the right to make their own choice."

After winning the governorship, Romney agreed not to expand or contract the state's pro-choice laws, preferring to maintain the status quo. When I asked him why he chose to sit out
the fight over one of the most important issues of the day, he
replied that he preferred to focus on other issues that he had
chosen as his platform. When I pressed him on whether he
should have displayed more leadership on the abortion issue,
Romney said: "You decide which of the things that you're
going to take and you're going to fight for. And that's exactly
what I did."

In 2004, the year after he quietly began laying the foundation for a possible presidential bid, Romney announced that his
position on abortion had changed from pro-choice to pro-life.
Critics immediately accused him of flip-flopping in order to
shore up his conservative credentials in advance of his White
House campaign. But Romney insisted he had experienced a
genuine epiphany on abortion. He said it occurred during a
discussion on stem cell research legislation with a pair of experts from Harvard.

"At one point, one of the two said, 'This is not a moral issue
because we kill the embryos at fourteen days,' " Romney told
me. "And I looked over at Beth Myers, my chief of staff, and
we both had exactly the same reaction, which is it just hit us
hard. And as they walked out, I said, 'Beth, we have cheapened
the sanctity of life by virtue of the *Roe* v. *Wade* mentality.' And
from that point forward, I said to the people of Massachusetts: I

will continue to honor what I pledged to you, but I prefer to call myself pro-life."

As governor, Romney was constantly fighting attempts by the legislature to further undermine protection of the unborn. He told me that bills reached his desk asserting that "we're going to define life as beginning upon implantation. Now, you think about that. Under Massachusetts law, you're going to be able to combine sperm and eggs in the laboratory, grow it for heaven knows how long, and say it's never human, which it is. I called it Orwellian—maybe it's Huxley instead. It's a brave new world."

I asked Romney about his shifting stance on abortion during an August 2006 interview at the governor's office in Boston.

"My position has changed," he acknowledged.

But he made clear that the change was limited to his public policy on abortion, not his personal belief.

"I believe that life begins at conception. That's not a changed view," he stated unequivocally. "I am a purist—if it's life, it's life."

And yet Romney seemed to contradict this assertion just five months later, when he gave a speech in Washington. He was trying to explain to an audience of conservatives how his position on abortion had been altered by the stem cell debate.

"I hadn't given a lot of thought to when life began—I have to be honest with you—until this whole stem cell research matter came to the fore in our state and this bill came to my desk," Romney said on January 27.

This seemed at odds with Romney's earlier assertion that his life-begins-at-conception conviction was "not a changed view," which implied he had always felt this way. But if he had always believed that life begins at conception, why would he say that he "hadn't given a lot of thought to when life began" until 2004, when he was fifty-seven years old?

I decided to ask Romney for an explanation.

"How does a smart, religious father of five, grandfather many times over, who gets to be into his late fifties, who has run for Senate, run for governor in races in which abortion was an issue, how do you not give a lot of thought at that stage of your life, to when life begins?"

Romney's reply only further complicated his abortion stance.

"I've given a lot of thought to abortion and about being pro-choice or pro-life and what position to take. A lot of angst I've felt over the years about that issue. And as to when life begins, from the standpoint of the law, prior to the stem cell research debate, I'm not sure that— —I'm just trying to think when that became a major—"

As Romney trailed off about legal distinctions, I tried to bring him back to the question of morality.

"It seems to me that that is something that might occur to people—when life begins," I said. "I mean, some people believe that life begins at conception; some people believe it begins at birth; some people believe it is somewhere in between that. The fact that you said, 'I hadn't given a lot of thought to when life began,' struck me."

"There's no question but that a fetus is life," Romney said. "The question was, well, does the life begin at conception? Does it begin at implantation?"

Without pausing to answer these questions, Romney plowed ahead.

"I was, in my own life, very opposed to abortion. And yet I had this question," he said. "Is that something the government should decide? So I had this, if you will, a conflict that exists, when you're personally opposed to abortion, and then you're saying, 'Well, I'll let the law exist as it is; it's settled.' "

"But within that conflict, didn't you have an idea of when life began," I persisted, "aside from looking at the legalities?"

"The abortion debate didn't really hinge around when life began," Romney said. "Meaning, does it begin at day one, at conception? Or does it begin at day fourteen? The abortions were happening throughout almost a nine-month period."

Unlike countless defenders and opponents of abortion, who for decades have argued passionately over the precise moment in that nine-month period when life begins, Romney was telling me he never fretted over this line of demarcation.

"It wasn't a matter of when did life begin. I'm opposed to abortion—period. So it precludes the question," he said. "When does life begin? With abortion, there's no question: 'Well, gosh, what happens if she aborts at day two?' Well, you can't abort at day two because you don't know if you're pregnant until at least fifteen days or so. So when life began was never an issue on abortion."

This seemed yet another contradiction. Despite Romney's assertion that life begins at conception, he was now insisting "you can't abort at day two" or even on day fourteen, since it was impossible to ascertain pregnancy at that early stage. Yet pro-lifers believed that countless women performed such abortions every day by taking the "morning-after" pill, which destroys a fertilized embryo by preventing it from implanting in the womb if taken within three days after intercourse. In fact, as governor, Romney had tried in vain to block the morning-after pill from being distributed in Massachusetts without a prescription. In a letter to state lawmakers in 2005, he pointed out that the pill can "prevent the implantation of the embryo. To those who believe that life begins at conception, the morning-after pill can destroy the human life that was created at the moment of fertilization."

While Romney seemed ambivalent about the significance of life's start vis-à-vis the abortion debate, he was certain of its importance in other debates.

"With stem cell research, and particularly cloning," he told me, "that became the entire focus of the debate."

As part of Romney's pro-life epiphany, he ended up taking a dim view of stem cell research, especially the sort that amounted to what he called "creating life to destroy life." Yet his nuanced position on the issue placed him to the left of President Bush, who took a harder line against creating human embryos for the purpose of extracting their stem cells. Advocates of the practice argued that research on these stem cells might lead to cures for diseases such as multiple sclerosis. Ironically, Ann Romney was diagnosed with MS in 1998, which served to inoculate her husband somewhat against charges of pandering to conservatives on the stem cell issue.

The final component of Romney's pro-life epiphany was the issue of human cloning, which he concluded was wrong. Although the practice involved fertilizing an egg with a human clone cell instead of sperm, Romney said the results were the same.

"The second you put those together, you now have human life," Romney told me. "Therefore, to protect the sanctity of life in a civilized society, I will protect it from that point forward. And I'll let the theologians discuss when the soul enters that body. But that's a different matter that I'm not going to allow to enter into my definition of how we respect the sanctity of human life."

Nonetheless, Romney proceeded to wade into a theological discussion.

"From the standpoint of a religious context, I don't know when the spirit, or the soul, enters the body. And I haven't tried to calculate that," he told me. "My friend, [Utah Senator] Orrin Hatch, who's a strong member of my faith, says, 'Mitt, you're wrong. The spirit doesn't enter the body until much later.' And he says, 'Mitt you know that, religiously, from the church. Our church doesn't think the spirit enters that early.' "

Romney told me, "That's bringing religion into the argument." And while he accepts "all of the teachings of my church," Romney made clear those teachings would not overrule his public policy positions.

"Our church thinks that the spirit doesn't enter until much later," he said. "I'm not looking at a religious definition of life. I'm looking at a civilization's, at a civilized society's definition of when life begins."

THE MORMON FACTOR

Romney's shifting position on abortion is not the biggest obstacle to his presidential candidacy. His biggest obstacle is his religion. Mormonism looks suspiciously like a cult to some evangelical Christians, a crucial voting bloc in presidential elections.

"I think there will always be some people who will say I don't want to vote for someone who is of a different faith than mine," Romney told me. "That's fine, that's their right. And there will be some who say I want to vote for him *because* he is a good strong member of his church. So maybe it balances."

Not likely. The antipathy toward Mormonism goes well beyond the garden-variety skepticism that most Americans harbor toward unfamiliar religions. Numerous national polls show a significant portion of the American electorate simply would not vote for a Mormon as president. I asked Romney to make sense of this widespread mistrust of his faith.

"Well, I think it's less well known than other faiths," he said. "Its history as a religion has given an image that is not accurate, but is of some concern to some people. Certainly, the practice of polygamy in the 1800s is something that my church is going to take a long time to outlive."

The issue is further complicated by the fact that Mormonism is often confused with other sects that still practice polygamy. In 2006, HBO began airing *Big Love,* a TV drama about Utah polygamists. That same year, polygamy made headlines when authorities arrested Warren Steed Jeffs, who was on the FBI's Most Wanted List. Jeffs was the leader of the Fundamen-

talist Church of Jesus Christ of Latter-day Saints, a monicker
that is confusingly close to the Mormon Church's official name,
the Church of Jesus Christ of Latter-day Saints.

Such developments make it more difficult for Romney to
disabuse the public of the misconception that his church allows
plural marriage.

"I think there are a lot of people in this country who still
think members of my church practice or condone polygamy,"
Romney told me. "It bothers me no end that the term 'polygamy' keeps being associated with my faith. There is nothing
more awful, in my view, than the violation of the marriage cov-
enant that one has with one's wife. The practice of polygamy is
abhorrent, it's awful, and it drives me nuts that people who are
polygamists keep pretending to use the umbrella of my church.
My church abhors it, it excommunicates people who practice it,
and it's got nothing to do with my faith."

As for those who mistakenly believe that Mormonism con-
dones polygamy, Romney says their reluctance to vote for him
is understandable.

"I would not want a president of the United States who
practiced or in the back of his mind was in favor of polygamy,"
he said. "So I understand why people have that view, in some
cases. And hopefully, as time goes on and I become more prominent in this race, people will recognize, 'OK, he doesn't believe
that and his church doesn't believe that either.' And that will
take down some of the concern."

Some of Romney's supporters have urged him not to get
drawn into a theological discussion of his religion. They say it
would be akin to a Catholic presidential candidate, such as

Rudy Giuliani, being asked to explain transubstantiation, the Catholic belief that bread and wine are transformed literally into the body and blood of Jesus at daily Mass.

"It's a mistake for me to go through all of the teachings in my church and say: Do you believe this one? Do you believe that one? Do you believe that one?" Romney told me. "It's not so much because I'm afraid to say that I believe those things. It's instead because I think I open the door to an area of inquiry that should not be part of a presidential election.

"So what I would prefer to do is to say: I believe in my church and I'm not a cafeteria member of my church," he said. "I accept the teachings of my church and so that assumes all of the teachings of my church. And I'm not going to go through one by one and describe each teaching."

Still, Romney told me he would probably need to give a major address about Mormonism, just as John F. Kennedy gave one about Catholicism, to assure Americans that as president, he will not take orders from church authorities. So while Romney seeks to avoid discussing the particular theological tenets of Mormonism, he expects to address general questions about the intersection of religion and public policy. He even anticipates specific queries.

" 'Would you go to the church leadership to ask their opinion on an important issue?' The answer is no, I would not. 'If you were to receive a call from the church leadership with a view on an issue, would you accept the call?' No, I would not."

Why not?

"Because I believe in a separation between a person who is a secular leader and the hierarchy of a church," Romney told me.

"And so I can describe those things without getting into: 'Do you believe the leaders of your church are inspired?' Well, of course I do. 'Well, if you believe they're inspired, then why wouldn't you take their advice on what you should do in Iraq?' And so, in my opinion, a presidential candidate is unwise to open that area of inquiry because it prejudices future candidates well beyond myself."

Besides, Romney does not expect the unique attributes of Mormonism to affect his presidency.

"For the life of me, I can't imagine a setting or an issue that I would approach or think about differently than would a good evangelical or a good Catholic or a good Presbyterian. Someone might be able to think up one, but I haven't been able to think of that.

"Now, there are differences between my faith and other faiths. For instance, our church says that Mormons shouldn't drink alcohol. But it's not because alcohol is somehow evil. It's more, you know, for my health and as a show of faith. As governor, I had no problem whatsoever signing laws allowing sales of alcohol on Sunday, although that didn't used to be the law.

"So it's not like you in any way think that the distinctive qualities of your religion somehow affect public policy. They really don't. The distinctive qualities of my religion have very little, if anything, to do with public policy that I can think of."

And yet in general terms, Romney is convinced that a religious leader, regardless of denomination, would make a better president than an atheist.

"You would hope that a person of deep faith would have a higher standard of ethical conduct, honesty, integrity, willingness to honor their commitments than somebody who didn't feel the same sense of moral obligation. But I'm not sure I can prove that, based on conduct over the last few years in Washington," he told me with a laugh.

"My faith has made me a better person than I would have been. Far from perfect, but better than I would have been. And I think that's true of virtually every other faith in the world. If you follow the principles, if you live the principles of your faith, it will make you a better person. And it would make you more likely to be honest, not dishonest; more likely to be concerned with the interests of other people; more likely to honor your obligations. And that will make you a more effective leader."

I noted that President Bush, an evangelical Christian, says he draws serenity from his faith, which helps him persevere through the enormous trials and tribulations of his office. Bush told me he believes in "the power of faith to bring comfort in times of turbulence." But Romney hinted that, if anything, religion might play a lesser role in his own presidency.

"There's a perhaps apocryphal story, but widespread in my church, about the second president of my church, Brigham Young, at a time when a wagon train was crossing the North Platte River," Romney told me. "One of the wagons broke loose and started to float down the river. The team of oxen was unable to pull the wagon. And the driver of the wagon got on his knees and started to pray. And Brigham Young rode his horse out into the middle of the river and grabbed the guy and said: 'This is no time for prayer.'"

Romney laughed at the story, but said it contained a lot of truth about Mormonism.

"In my faith, there is a very strong sense of 'it's up to you,' "
he told me. "God put us here, but he doesn't run things like a
puppeteer. And if I'm messing things up, I can't go back and
say, 'OK, God, you take care of it.' It's on me.

"I think there is a sense of fatalism that some people carry,
whether it's religious or nonreligious, but that probably is not a
productive thing. I think you have to assume that everything's
in your hands and you hope that if you mess up that somehow,
something good will come of it. But it's going to be in your
hands."

Romney once wrote that some Americans "thought us Mormons to be too goody-two-shoes." He explained to me that this
"clean-cut image" comes from the church's embrace of "old-
fashioned American" values, which run counter to those of the
"MTV generation."

"Mormons don't smoke and drink and don't believe in
sex outside of marriage—premarital sex or extramarital sex—
and that's a little unusual today," he told me. "And then of
course you have all the young missionaries going around wearing the suits and ties and little badges on bicycles. That's not
exactly a Prince—the artist formerly known as Prince—kind
of image."

He added: "The church told membership that tattoos are
like graffiti on your body. I mean, the church is pretty conservative, if you will, when it comes to manners of fashion, and
the like. It tells people to dress modestly and so forth, it tells
girls not to date before they're sixteen."

In the end, Romney is betting that evangelical Christians

will focus more on their theological commonalities with Mormons than their differences.

"I believe in God, I believe in Jesus Christ as my savior," he told me in his Boston campaign headquarters in 2007. "I'm sure there are differences between the doctrines of my church and the doctrines of other churches that believe in God and Jesus Christ."

He added: "But I do believe that the values which are part of my heritage are very much the American values that people look for in a leader. And that's why in a state like this one, which is 55 percent Catholic, they wondered about a Mormon guy, but quickly recognized that the values that I have are very much the values of people of faith throughout the land."

Romney's wife, Ann, once joked that among the top contenders for the GOP presidential nomination, only her husband, the Mormon, had limited himself to one wife. It was a sly reference to the fact that Rudy Giuliani and Newt Gingrich each have had three wives, while John McCain and Fred Thompson each have had two. By contrast, if Romney is elected, during his first year in office, he will observe the fortieth anniversary of his marriage to his high-school sweetheart. In a not-so-veiled swipe at Giuliani, McCain, and Gingrich, all of whom fell for younger women while still married, Romney told me that "people who commit adultery or other practices of that nature are carrying out absolutely heinous acts."

Romney also opposes gay marriage more vigorously than any other top presidential candidate in either party. While he was governor, Massachusetts became the only state in the nation to allow gay couples to legally marry. Romney tried to overturn the law, but was stymied by the state's liberal supreme court and overwhelmingly Democratic legislature. Unlike McCain and Giuliani, Romney favors a constitutional amendment defining marriage as between a man and a woman.

"I believe that traditional marriage between a man and a woman is the best course because I believe that on average, the children in a society will be more prepared for their lives if they have the benefit of a mom and a dad," he told me. "There are some great single moms and some great grandmas, and my guess is there are probably some great gay couples that are raising a child. But overall, as a society, we prefer a setting where there is a male and a female associated with the development of a child."

To Romney, that basic building block of society transcends the whims of government.

"Family's been here from the beginning, it was ordained of divinity, and it should be protected for the strengthening of a society. Much of our legal system flows, if you will, from the foundation of biblical commandments, and I think our secular society has forgotten that and has subsumed those values. But it's still part of the Western culture and the Western heritage that came from our biblical roots."

Like George W. Bush in 2000, Mitt Romney says he will not be personally devastated if he loses the White House in 2008.

"I've had my career," he told me. "I was a successful business leader. I'm a pretty successful dad and a successful husband. Those are the things that are most meaningful to me.

And I'm putting myself forward because I think I could be a very good president for this country.

"But if we choose somebody else who could be a very good president, I'll feel fine," he concluded. "This is not defining who I am."

WHERE MITT ROMNEY STANDS
ON THE ISSUES

ABORTION
He now says: "I'm firmly pro-life." But in 2002, when he ran for governor of Massachusetts, he said: "I believe women should have the right to make their own choice."

CLIMATE CHANGE
Supports voluntary cuts in greenhouses gases, although he is not convinced that global warming exists or that it is caused by man.

GAY MARRIAGE
Supports a constitutional ban.

HEALTH CARE
Pushed through mandatory health insurance for all residents of Massachusetts.

IMMIGRATION

Opposes any guest worker program until the borders have been secured.

IRAQ

Generally supports President Bush's policy, although he has criticized missteps by the administration.

TAXES

Kept a campaign pledge not to raise taxes as governor of Massachusetts. In 2004, his call for a tax cut was rejected by the Democratic legislature.

2

HILLARY RODHAM CLINTON

"**I**'m probably the most famous person you don't really know."

That's how Hillary Rodham Clinton chose to describe herself just days after formally entering the presidential race in early 2007. While it may have sounded like a whimsical, throwaway line, it was every bit as calculated as the rest of Hillary's public persona. That's because the junior senator from New York knows she must redefine herself if she wants to succeed in her White House bid. Already saddled with dangerously high unfavorability ratings, the former First Lady is hoping for a second chance to make a first impression. It will not be easy, since the overwhelming majority of Americans made up their minds about Hillary long before she entered the presidential race. Some love her, others despise her, but very few remain undecided. Hillary's job is to convince those persuadable voters to forget all the nasty things they may have heard about her.

"If you could pick an adjective that you hope people would use to describe you, what would it be?" Hillary was asked on ABC.

"Real," she replied. "I think that when you've been in the public eye as long as I have and you are basically viewed through so many different lenses, there has been kind of a cottage industry trying to turn me into a caricature of who I am."

Who, then, is the real Hillary Rodham Clinton? Is she the steely-eyed hawk who voted for the Iraq War? Or the antiwar dove who now vows to end it? Although Hillary is rated as a solid liberal by interest groups on both sides of the aisle, she has carefully cultivated the image of a moderate. This has been accomplished largely through her 2002 vote to authorize the war in Iraq. Yet that vote has also become the biggest stumbling block on her road to the White House.

Actually, with Hillary, it's more of a return trip. Having already spent eight years at 1600 Pennsylvania Avenue as First Lady, Hillary is determined to make history as the first woman president in American history.

FROM GOLDWATER GIRL TO CAMPUS LIBERAL

Hillary Diane Rodham was born in Chicago on October 26, 1947, the first child of Dorothy, a homemaker, and her husband, Hugh, a textile executive. In 1950, Hillary's brother Hugh was born and the Rodhams moved to the affluent suburb of Park Ridge, where the family's third and final child, Tony, joined the Rodhams in 1954.

"My mother was basically a Democrat, although she kept it quiet in Republican Park Ridge," Hillary wrote in her 2003 autobiography, *Living History*. "My dad was a rock-ribbed, up-by-your-bootstraps, conservative Republican and proud of it. He was also tight-fisted with money."

From a very young age, Hillary was keenly aware of national politics. In 1960, while still in the eighth grade, she rooted for Richard Nixon to win the presidential election. She was outraged by his narrow loss to John F. Kennedy, which was linked to voting irregularities in her native Chicago.

Between 1961 and 1968, Hillary was influenced by a number of people who would gradually transform her from a conservative Republican "Goldwater Girl" to a liberal Democrat who reveled in campus protests. The first of these was the Reverend Don Jones, who in 1961 was hired as the new youth minister at Hillary's church, First Methodist in Park Ridge. The leftist cleric would be fired by the church within two years, but not before planting the seeds of liberalism in the impressionable Hillary. At one point Jones took Hillary and the rest of the youth group to hear Martin Luther King Jr. speak in Chicago.

Still, Hillary supported conservative Republican Barry Goldwater's run against Democratic president Lyndon Johnson in 1964. Goldwater wasn't the only one who lost a presidential election that year. So did Hillary, who ran unsuccessfully for president of her public high school in Park Ridge. Unfazed, she headed off to Massachusetts to attend Wellesley College, a small, all-women's liberal arts school outside of Boston.

"I arrived at Wellesley carrying my father's political beliefs and my mother's dreams and left with the beginnings of my own," she wrote in *Living History*.

But the academic rigors of college nearly overwhelmed Hillary, who informed her parents in October 1965, shortly after beginning her first semester, that she was not smart enough for the school. Her father urged her to persevere and eventually Hillary became a strong student. She also became active in extracurricular groups.

Hillary was elected president of Wellesley's Young Republicans club as a freshman. But after months of lectures by liberal professors, she quit the post before the school year ended. That summer, she worked as a research assistant for political science instructor Anthony D'Amato, who was later fired by Wellesley for his stridently left-wing views, according to author Gail Sheehy in *Hillary's Choice*.

It wasn't long before Hillary saw advantages in the absence of male students at Wellesley.

"It was a given that the president of the class, the editor of the paper, and the top student in every field would be a woman," she marveled. "And it could be any of us."

Having lost her high-school presidency race to a boy, Hillary decided to try her luck against the girls of Wellesley. She campaigned to discontinue mandatory prayer in the dining hall and replace letter grades with a pass-fail system. These proved to be popular positions and Hillary won the Wellesley student presidency in February 1968.

She also found time to volunteer for the presidential campaign of antiwar senator Eugene McCarthy, who was challenging President Lyndon Johnson for the Democratic nomination. On weekends, Hillary would travel to New Hampshire, where McCarthy managed to throw a scare into Johnson in the Democratic primary of March 1968, although the nomination would eventually go to Hubert Humphrey.

That summer, Hillary somewhat reluctantly accepted an internship, arranged by Wellesley, at the House Republican Conference in Washington. She then parlayed the internship into a trip to Miami Beach, Florida, for the Republican National Convention. Hillary worked on behalf of liberal Republican Nelson Rockefeller, who came up short in his third bid for the GOP presidential nomination.

"The nomination of Richard Nixon cemented the ascendance of a conservative over a moderate ideology within the Republican Party, a dominance that has only grown more pronounced over the years as the party has continued its move to the right and moderates have dwindled in numbers and influence," Hillary wrote in *Living History*. "I sometimes think that I didn't leave the Republican Party as much as it left me."

Later that summer, Hillary attended the Democratic National Convention in Chicago before returning to Wellesley for her senior year. She decided to write her senior thesis on radical leftist Saul Alinsky, a community organizer in Chicago who would also have a deep influence on Hillary's future rival for the Democratic presidential nomination, Barack Obama. Alinsky offered to hire Hillary as soon as she finished her senior year, but she already had plans to attend law school at Yale.

On May 31, 1969, Hillary became the first student at Wellesley to deliver a speech to the graduating class at commencement. She began her speech by rebutting the Republican commencement speaker, African-American senator Edward Brooke of Massachusetts, a move that irritated Wellesley president Ruth Adams. Hillary then segued into a somewhat rambling, overwrought oration about "the burden of an inauthentic reality." The speech, even allowing for the youthful angst of the era, bordered on pretentious.

"Words have a funny way of trapping our minds on the way to our tongues, but there are necessary means—even in this multimedia age—for attempting to come to grasps with some of the inarticulate, maybe even inarticulable, things that we're feeling," she mused. "We are, all of us, exploring a world that none of us even understands, and attempting to create within that uncertainty. But there are some things we feel, feelings that our prevailing, acquisitive, and competitive corporate life, including tragically the universities, is not the way of life for us. We're searching for more immediate, ecstatic and penetrating mode of living. And so our questions, our questions about our institutions, about our colleges, about our churches, about our government, continue."

Excerpts of the speech, along with a photo of the speaker, appeared in the June 1969 issue of *Life* magazine. Hillary had gone national. But the heady experience was mitigated somewhat by her job that summer—cleaning the guts from salmon at a fish-processing plant in Valdez, Alaska.

"Of all the jobs I've had, sliming fish was pretty good preparation for life in Washington," she later wrote in her autobiography.

ENTER BILL CLINTON

In 1970, Hillary met a fellow Yale law student named Bill Clinton from Arkansas.

"With Hillary, there was no arm's length," Bill wrote in his autobiography, *My Life*. "She was in my face from the start, and, before I knew it, in my heart."

By the summer of 1971, Hillary and Bill were living together in a tiny apartment off the Berkeley campus of the University of California. After completing a summer stint at a small law firm, Hillary returned to Yale and moved into a small apartment with Bill. The place was owned by fellow Yalie Greg Craig, who would go on to defend President Bill Clinton during his impeachment trial in the Senate.

By 1972, Hillary was working at the Children's Defense Fund, a liberal advocacy group in Washington. But she left the job to accompany Bill to Austin, Texas, so they could work for the presidential campaign of liberal Democrat George McGovern. They befriended a political operative named Betsey Wright, who would one day be tasked with quashing "bimbo eruptions" during Bill Clinton's presidential campaign. Although McGovern lost to Nixon in a landslide, the experience was formative for Hillary and Bill.

"That 1972 campaign was our first rite of passage," Hillary recalled in *Living History*.

After graduating from law school in 1973, Hillary and Bill visited Great Britain, where Bill proposed. Hillary begged off, telling him, "No, not now."

"I knew that when I decided to marry, I wanted it to be for life," she wrote in *Living History*. "I thought of him as a force of nature . . . and wondered whether I'd be up to the task of living through his seasons."

So they tried a long-distance relationship. Bill moved to Fayetteville, Arkansas, to teach at the University of Arkansas and plan the launch of his political career. Hillary moved to Cambridge, Massachusetts, to resume working for the Children's Defense Fund. But she would not remain there long.

In 1974, Hillary, now twenty-six, moved to Washington to join the staff of a House inquiry into possible impeachment proceedings against Nixon. She researched the history of impeachment cases, diagramed the hierarchy of the Nixon White House, listened to the subpoenaed tapes of Nixon's White House conversations, and helped devise procedural rules for the House Judiciary Committee. But her work came to halt on August 9, when Nixon resigned, precluding impeachment.

Although Hillary had flunked the bar exam in Washington, D.C., she passed the one in Arkansas, where Bill was living. So she moved in with him in Fayetteville.

"I had fallen in love with Bill in law school and wanted to be with him," she wrote in *Living History*. "I knew I was always happier with Bill than without him, and I'd always assumed that I could live a fulfilling life anywhere. If I was going to grow as a person, I knew it was time for me—to paraphrase Eleanor Roosevelt—to do what I was most afraid to do."

Following in Bill's footsteps, Hillary took a job teaching at the University of Arkansas. The couple had audacious ambitions, according to *Her Way,* a 2007 biography of Hillary by *New York Times* reporters Jeff Gerth and Don Van Natta Jr.

"Though still unwed, Hillary and Bill had already made a secret pact of ambition, one whose contours and importance to the two of them has remained their secret all across these years," the reporters wrote. "They agreed to embark on a political partnership with two staggering goals: revolutionize the Democratic Party and, at the same time, capture the presidency for Bill. They called it their 'twenty-year project,' an auspicious timetable for two young people in their midtwenties. And they agreed that they only way they would be able to achieve these goals was to do whatever it took to win elections and defeat their opponents. Bill would be the project's public face, of course. And Hillary would serve as the enterprise's behind-the-scenes manager and enforcer."

She married the future president on October 11, 1975, but decided to retain her maiden name, Hillary Rodham, instead of adopting the Clinton moniker. She considered herself a feminist.

By this time, the couple's first attempt at winning an election had ended in failure when Bill lost his bid for a congressional seat in November 1974. But two years later, he was elected attorney general of Arkansas. So the couple moved from Fayetteville to Little Rock, the state capital, where Hillary went to work for the Rose law firm.

She soon found herself representing big business in a case against an advocate for the poor, the Association of Community Organizations for Reform Now (ACORN). Hillary convinced a judge to reverse ACORN's successful ballot initiative that required Little Rock utilities to lower rates for residential customers while boosting them for businesses. She had already moved away from the idealism of her Wellesley speech, in which she railed that the "competitive corporate life" was "not the way of life for us."

By 1978, Hillary was so deeply into the "competitive corporate life" that she bought one thousand dollars in cattle futures and watched it turn into one hundred thousand dollars in the space of nine months. The highly unusual deal would be thrown back in her face years later, when Hillary railed against the 1980s as the Republican "decade of greed." Still, she never acknowledged wrongdoing.

"It was very big money for me and my family," she conceded to reporters. Yet she insisted, "There isn't any evidence that anybody gave me any favorable treatment."

Also in 1978, Hillary took an even more fateful step that, in the world of Clinton scandals, would make the cattle futures flap look like child's play. She and Bill entered into a partnership with some friends, Jim and Susan McDougal, to buy 230 acres of land along a remote stretch of the White River in Arkansas. The deal, sealed with $203,000 in bank loans and no money down, was known as Whitewater. Hillary would later rue the day she and Bill became entangled with Whitewater, calling it the "only stupid dumb thing we ever did."

In 1978, with the help of Hillary and political strategist Dick Morris, Bill Clinton was elected governor of Arkansas. Hillary was now the First Lady of Arkansas. But she kept her day job at Rose and even became the firm's first female partner in 1979. By now she had become close friends with two other partners in the firm, Webb Hubbell and Vince Foster. Her long hours at work, coupled with the birth of her daughter, Chelsea, in early 1980, prevented her from spending much time on Bill's re-election campaign, which he lost in November 1980. It turned out his tax hike on auto registrations had angered voters.

Hillary decided it was time for drastic action. In another ideological concession to the political ambitions she harbored for her husband, she decided to add the name Clinton to Hillary Rodham.

"I learned the hard way," she wrote in *Living History,* "that some voters in Arkansas were seriously offended by the fact that I kept my maiden name." She added: "I decided it was more important for Bill to be governor again than for me to keep my maiden name."

Armed with her new name and able to spend more time on her husband's comeback, Hillary helped Bill regain the governor's mansion in 1982. He would remain in office for the next decade, a period when the seeds of additional scandals would be sown.

By this time, Jim McDougal had purchased a savings and loan, named it Madison Guaranty, and begun using it to prop up the struggling Whitewater venture. The plot thickened in 1985, when McDougal hired Hillary as Madison's lawyer. This meant the governor's wife was representing the governor's business partner in dealings with state regulators who were appointed by the governor. This ethical morass caught up with Hillary in 1986, when she was forced to refund all fees from state-related work she performed at Rose. That same year, she took over the administration of the Whitewater venture from McDougal, who was removed from Madison by federal regulators. McDougal was eventually indicted for fraud, although he was ultimately acquitted. Still, Hillary would later lament that "Whitewater was a fiasco."

This failed real estate venture was not the only project keeping Hillary busy during this period. Upon retaking the governor's mansion, Bill had appointed Hillary to head up an effort to reform the state's public schools. To this end, Hillary and Bill decided to raise the state's sales tax.

Meanwhile, Hillary was named to the boards of several liberal advocacy groups, including the Children's Defense Fund and the New World Foundation. She also became the first female member of Wal-Mart's board of directors.

STANDING BY HER MAN

Hillary was not blind to the fact that her husband was unfaithful to her. In fact, she helped him seek political inoculation against the adultery issue in advance of his first run for the White House. In September 1991, the couple met with a group of influential newspaper reporters in Washington, where Bill allowed that "our relationship has not been perfect or free of difficulties."

Four months later, as Bill was seeking the Democratic presidential nomination, it was revealed that he had an affair with a woman named Gennifer Flowers, who had tape-recorded their phone conversations. To contain the scandal, Bill and

Hillary appeared on CBS immediately after the 1992 Super Bowl, when an enormous audience was tuned to *60 Minutes*. Without getting into specifics, Bill admitted "causing pain in my marriage." Hillary was decidedly less conciliatory.

"You know, I'm not sitting here, some little woman standing by my man like Tammy Wynette," she snapped. "I'm standing here because I love him and respect him and honor what he's been through and what we've been through together. And you know, if that's not enough for people, then heck, don't vote for him."

For many Americans, this was their first glimpse of Hillary Rodham Clinton. The reaction was largely negative. Hillary was even forced to apologize to the deeply offended Wynette.

Seven weeks later, Hillary solidified her reputation as a hard-edged feminist with an even more acerbic remark. It was prompted by former California governor Jerry Brown, who was challenging Bill for the Democratic presidential nomination. During a debate in Chicago, Brown accused the Clintons of a "conflict of interest" because Bill was "funneling money to his wife's law firm as state business." The next morning, Hillary shot back: "I suppose I could have stayed home and baked cookies and had teas. What I decided to do was fulfill my profession, which I entered before my husband was in public life."

One of Bill's political advisers, Paul Begala, warned Hillary that the remark would be perceived as "an attack on stay-at-home moms." Hillary replied: "You worry too much." But Begala was right; the backlash was significant. In another accommodation to the political ambitions of Bill, the feminist

Hillary cheerfully began touting cookie recipes in an attempt
to undo the damage.

Of course, Bill ended up winning the 1992 election and Hillary became the nation's First Lady. But instead of setting up
her offices in the East Wing of the White House, the traditional
domain of First Ladies, Hillary insisted on office space in the
West Wing. There she created what she called "Hillaryland," a
staff of fiercely loyal and protective advisers who placed a pre-
mium on secrecy. Hillary even convinced her alma mater,
Wellesley, to place her senior thesis under lock and key. Eager
to surround herself with praetorian guards who could be
trusted, she summoned to Washington her closest confidants
from Arkansas, including her Rose law partners, Vince Foster
and Webb Hubbell.

But when Bill deputized Hillary to chair the president's task
force on national health care reform, her penchant for secrecy
became a political liability. Several health care groups sued to
open up the deliberations of the task force to the public. But
Hillary insisted on secrecy for herself and liberal adviser Ira
Magaziner as they attempted what amounted to a government
takeover of 14 percent of the American economy. The initiative was off-putting to congressional Democrats who wouldn't
bring Hillary's health care reform bill to a vote in the House or
Senate.

"The quest ended in defeat in 1994 and led to her reputation
as a big-government liberal," the *New York Times* reported.

Hillary later admitted ignoring a "giant red flag" from
Congress that should have warned her that she was moving
"too quickly" on her initiative. Citing her "own missteps" in

"trying to do too much, too fast," she acknowledged that she "underestimated the resistance I would meet as a First Lady with a policy mission." Stung by the failure, she quietly resolved to take a piecemeal approach to the nationalization of health care.

"Some day we will fix the system," she wrote in *Living History*. "When we do, it will be the result of more than fifty years of efforts by Harry Truman, Richard Nixon, Jimmy Carter and Bill and me. Yes, I'm still glad we tried."

Health care was not the only setback Hillary suffered in her early tenure as First Lady. She also became embroiled in a number of significant scandals, starting with Travelgate. In May 1993, Hillary was widely accused of firing all seven staffers in the White House travel office and replacing them with family and friends from Arkansas. She swore under oath that she had not masterminded the firings, although her testimony was contradicted by David Watkins, the White House official tasked with carrying out the firings.

"We both knew there would be hell to pay [if] we failed to take swift and decisive action in conformity with the first lady's wishes," Watkins wrote in a memo to White House Chief of Staff Thomas McLarty.

The dispute triggered half a dozen investigations that culminated in a report by independent counsel Robert Ray more than seven years after the firings.

"The evidence is overwhelming that she in fact did have a role in the decision to fire the employees," Ray concluded. "Thus, her statement to the contrary under oath to this Office was factually false."

But "factually false" was not the same as "knowingly false," Ray conceded.

"The evidence was insufficient to prove to a jury beyond a reasonable doubt that any of Mrs. Clinton's statements and testimony regarding her involvement in the travel office firings were knowingly false," the prosecutor wrote. "Accordingly, the independent counsel has declined prosecution of Mrs. Clinton."

Two months after the travel office employees were fired, deputy White House counsel Vince Foster committed suicide. The tragedy shocked Hillary, who had been Foster's law partner and close friend at the Rose law firm in Arkansas. Foster had been questioned by investigators in the Travelgate probe. His White House portfolio had included serving as point man on Hillary's controversial involvement in Madison Guaranty. Consequently, Foster was under enormous stress, as evidenced by his suicide note, the torn-up pieces of which were found at the bottom of his briefcase.

"I was not meant for the job in the spotlight of Washington," Foster wrote. "Here, ruining people is considered sport."

After the funeral, Hillary remarked to Webb Hubbell, who had been installed as the number-three lawyer at the Justice Department, that "we shouldn't have asked him to come to Washington," Hubbell later recounted in his book, *Friends in High Places.*

Foster's death would give rise to what Hillary called "a cottage industry of conspiracy theorists and investigators trying to prove that Vince was murdered to cover up what he 'knew about Whitewater.' "

"A VAST, RIGHT-WING CONSPIRACY"

Six months later, as scandals raged in the White House, Attorney General Janet Reno appointed an independent counsel, Robert Fiske, to investigate Whitewater and Madison Guaranty. Hillary bitterly opposed the move, but Bill calculated that the probe would clear them once and for all.

Within two months of Fiske's appointment, Hubbell resigned as associate attorney general. He was accused of defrauding his former partners and clients at the Rose law firm. Hillary refused to believe the charges and even helped line up consulting jobs for him to defray the costs of his legal defense.

"We had no reason to disbelieve his denials of wrongdoing," Hillary told NPR's Diane Rehm. "He unequivocally just looked us in the eye and said, 'I didn't do anything wrong. This'll blow over. This is all being taken care of.' "

But by the end of the year, Hubbell admitted to stealing hundreds of thousands of dollars from his partners and clients. He pleaded guilty to felony counts of tax evasion and mail fraud and went to prison for eighteen months. Another Hillary friend had been felled by scandal.

That same year, a woman named Paula Jones publicly accused Bill Clinton of having sexually harrassed her when he was governor of Arkansas. Bill denied the charges, which rattled Hillary. Frustrated by the never-ending scandals, she resolved to find a journalist who would tell her side of the story. She invited James Stewart of the liberal magazine *New Yorker* to meet her in the White House.

"There were a few flashes of anger as she described her and

her husband's treatment by the media," Stewart later wrote. "She seemed especially upset by coverage of Paula Jones' sexual-harassment suit, mentioning that people had no idea how painful it was for her to endure public reports of her husband's alleged infidelity. She railed against the tactics of the right-wing media and think tanks, wondering how they were being financed. A recurring theme was that she couldn't understand why reporters would publish allegations by people of questionable integrity in the face of denials by her and her husband. The First Lady freely conceded that mistakes had been made and that she, in particular, had put too much emphasis on privacy, leading to perceptions that the White House had something to hide. This was not true, she insisted."

Nine days later, in an attempt to exhaust the media of all scandal inquiries, Hillary gave a lengthy press conference in the State Dining Room of the White House. It would become known as the "pink" press conference because she wore a pink sweater. Reporters grilled her on Whitewater, Madison, cattle futures, and the death of Vince Foster.

"Is there a fundamental distrust of the Clintons in America?" one reporter asked.

"Well, I hope not," Hillary replied. "I mean, that would be something that I would regret very much. I do think that we are transition figures, if you will. We don't fit easily into a lot of our pre-existing categories."

She went on to suggest that America might not be ready for a First Lady who was also a feminist, having worked all her life except for the four months after Chelsea's birth.

"Having been independent, having made decisions, it's a

little difficult for us as a country, maybe, to make the transition of having a woman—like many of the women in this room—sitting in this house," she told the reporters. "So I think that the standards—and to some extent, the expectations and the demands—have changed. And I'm trying to find my way through it and trying to figure out how best to be true to myself and how to fulfill my responsibilities to my husband and my daughter and the country."

Hillary acknowledged that her penchant for secrecy had sometimes backfired.

"I do feel like I've always been a fairly private person leading a public life," she said. "I've always believed in a zone of privacy. And I told a friend the other day that I feel after resisting for a long time, I've been rezoned."

Still, she couldn't shake the sense that she and her husband were being persecuted.

"We were being asked things and demands were being placed on us that had never been demanded of prior inhabitants of this house—unprecedented," she lamented. "I resisted it in ways that may have raised more questions than they answered. And I just don't think that was a very useful road for me to go down."

After the press conference ended, Hillary concluded that her efforts to placate journalists would never bear fruit.

"They're not going to let up," she told a friend. "They're just going to keep coming at us, no matter what we do."

In June 1994, Fiske subpoenaed Hillary's billing records of Madison from when she had worked at Rose. She claimed she didn't have them and didn't know where they were. Moreover, she began to believe that the focus on Clinton scandals was a political effort to undermine "the progressive agenda by any means."

"If you believed everything you heard on the airwaves in 1994, you would conclude that your President was a Communist, that the First Lady was a murderess and that together they had hatched a plot to take away your guns and force you to give up your family doctor (if you had one) for a Socialist health care system," she recalled in *Living History*.

Hillary reneged on her promise to cooperate with James Stewart, who nonetheless went on to write a book about the Clinton scandals, calling it *Blood Sport*. To make matters worse, the Democrats lost control of Congress in the midterm elections of 1994. Hillary was so despondent that she resumed her imaginary conversations with Eleanor Roosevelt, according to her autobiography.

On January 4, 1996, Hillary announced she had found the billing records from Rose law firm that prosecutors had subpoenaed more than eighteen months earlier. She had no explanation for how they had suddenly materialized on a table inside the White House residence. This was too much for *New York Times* columnist William Safire, who had voted for Bill Clinton.

"Americans of all political persuasions are coming to the sad realization that our First Lady—a woman of undoubted talents who was a role model for many in her generation—is a congenital liar," he wrote.

Most Americans agreed, according to a poll taken by CNN and *Time* magazine. Asked whether Hillary had lied about her role in Whitewater, 52 percent of respondents said yes, while only half that many, or 27 percent, said no.

Two weeks later, Hillary became the only First Lady in history to testify before a federal grand jury. But her legal problems paled in comparison to those of her husband, who was still being sued by Paula Jones.

"With the wisdom of hindsight, of course, not settling the Jones suit early on was the second biggest tactical mistake made in handling the barrage of investigations and lawsuits," Hillary wrote in her autobiography. "The first was requesting an independent counsel at all."

In a deposition on January 17, 1998, the president was grilled about Jones and other women, including a former White House intern named Monica Lewinsky. Although Clinton had engaged in sex with Lewinsky in the White House on numerous occasions, he now denied it under oath. Four days later, the Lewinsky scandal exploded across the front page of the *Washington Post*. Bill awakened Hillary and denied the affair. She claims she believed his denial, even if the rest of the country didn't.

"I had little trouble believing the accusations were groundless," she wrote in *Living History*.

Less than a week after the scandal broke, Hillary blamed it on a "vast, right-wing conspiracy" against her and her husband. As for their critics, Hillary shrugged, "Screw 'em!"

Month after month, the humiliating disclosures mounted. CBS's *60 Minutes* aired allegations that Bill had groped a woman named Kathleen Willey in the White House. Then came word that Lewinsky handed prosecutors a dress stained with Bill's semen. The president was reduced to giving a blood sample to investigators in the Map Room of the White House. Knowing that his lies were about to be exposed, the president finally admitted to Hillary his affair with Lewinsky, who was young enough to be their daughter.

"He couldn't tell me seven months ago, he said, because he was too ashamed to admit it, and he knew how angry and hurt I would be," Hillary recalled in *Living History*. "I could hardly breathe. Gulping for air, I started crying and yelling at him, 'What do you mean? What are you saying? Why did you lie to me?'

"I was furious and getting more so by the second. He just stood there saying over and over again, 'I'm sorry. I'm so sorry. I was trying to protect you and Chelsea.' I couldn't believe what I was hearing. Up until now I only thought that he'd been fool-ish for paying attention to the young woman and was con-vinced that he was being railroaded. I couldn't believe he would do anything to endanger our marriage and our family. I was dumbfounded, heartbroken and outraged that I'd believed him at all.

"Then I realized that Bill and I had to tell Chelsea. When I told him he had to do this, his eyes filled with tears. He had betrayed the trust in our marriage, and we both knew it might be an irreparable breach. And we had to tell Chelsea that he had lied to her too. These were terrible moments for all of us. I didn't know whether our marriage could—or should—survive such a stinging betrayal."

"This was the most devastating, shocking and hurtful experience of my life," she added. "What my husband did was morally wrong. So was lying to me and misleading the American people about it."

And yet within two weeks, Hillary had decided not to leave Bill.

"I loved him," she explained in her autobiography. "As his wife, I wanted to wring Bill's neck. But he was also my President, and I thought that, in spite of everything, Bill led America and the world in a way that I continued to support. No matter what he had done, I did not think any person deserved the abusive treatment he had received."

Hillary resolved to wage scorched earth warfare against Kenneth Starr, who had replaced Fiske as the special prosecutor.

"If men like Starr and his allies could ignore the Constitution and abuse power for ideological and malicious ends to topple a President, I feared for my country," she railed. "Bill's presidency, the institutional presidency and the integrity of the Constitution hung in the balance."

On December 19, 1998, Hillary stood by Bill's side in the Rose Garden after the House impeached him on one count of perjury to the grand jury and one count of obstructing justice. He was the first elected president in U.S. history to be impeached.

The case then moved to the Senate for a trial to determine whether the president should be removed from office. Hillary called the proceedings "a political farce." The Senate ended up deadlocking, 50–50, on the obstruction charge, while forty-five senators voted guilty on the perjury charge. Since sixty-seven votes were needed for a conviction, the president remained in office.

But when he appeared in the Rose Garden after his acquittal on February 12, 1999, Hillary was not at his side. Instead, she was meeting with adviser Harold Ickes about an audacious plan to run for a U.S. Senate seat that would soon be vacant in New York. It was time for Hillary to step out on her own.

I LOVE NEW YORK

There was no shortage of obstacles. For starters, Hillary had never actually lived in New York. On the other hand, neither had Robert F. Kennedy, who nonetheless won the Senate seat in 1964 and used it as a springboard to a presidential campaign. So the Clintons bought a house in Chappaqua, New York, for $1.7 million, after convincing their top political fundraiser, Terry McAuliffe, to put up $1.35 million as collateral.

Second, there was the matter of Hillary's husband. She worried that women voters would question her decision to "stay married to Bill." And yet there was no denying that Bill was a shrewd political strategist who could coach Hillary to handle a formidable opponent, Rudy Giuliani, the former federal prosecutor and mayor who had cleaned up New York City.

"For twenty years, we've gone where I wanted to go and done what I wanted to do," Bill said he told his wife. "I'll give you the next twenty years."

But Bill couldn't prevent his wife, who had never run for

elected office, from making a major gaffe in November 1999. During a visit to the West Bank, Hillary publicly appeared with Palestinian leader Yasser Arafat's wife, Suha, who accused Israel of deliberately unleashing "poisonous gas" on Palestinians. Hillary, who had been wearing headphones and listening to a translation of the remarks from Arabic to English, then kissed Suha. After Jewish voters expressed outrage, Hillary claimed she had heard a faulty translation and later wrote in *Living History:* "Had I been aware of her hateful words, I would have denounced them on the spot."

Yet the controversy paled in comparison to the tabloid headlines generated by Giuliani, who was in the midst of a messy extramarital affair. Down nine points in the polls, Giuliani announced in May 2000 that he was dropping out of the race because he had prostate cancer. His Republican replacement was Congressman Rick Lazio of Long Island, who doomed his own candidacy when he attacked Hillary too aggressively. It happened in a debate in Buffalo in September 2000, when Lazio got in Hillary's face and demanded that she sign a document swearing off unlimited "soft money" contributions. This came across as bullying, and Hillary won the election by a dozen points.

A few weeks before Hillary became the only First Lady in U.S. history to be sworn into the U.S. Senate, she landed an $8 million advance from Simon & Schuster to write her autobiography, *Living History.* She immediately purchased a $2.85 million mansion in Washington and embarked on a $1 million renovation that included installation of an elevator. Hillary was now a rich woman.

She also moved "Hillaryland" from the White House to Capitol Hill.

"My staff prided themselves on discretion, loyalty, and camaraderie, and we had our own special ethos," she later wrote. While Bill's staff "had a tendency to leak," she added, "Hillaryland never did."

On September 11, 2001, Hillary reacted to the terrorist attacks by pledging her support to President Bush.

"We are united behind the president," she said on CNN. "This is an attack on America and we will support the president in whatever steps he takes. We can't let these evil acts deter us. We are going to support the president."

The next day, on the Senate floor, she was even more outspoken in her support of Bush.

"We will also stand united behind our president as he and his advisers plan the necessary actions to demonstrate America's resolve and commitment," she vowed. "Not only to seek out an exact punishment on the perpetrators, but to make very clear that not only those who harbor terrorists, but those who in any way aid or comfort them whatsoever will now face the wrath of our country."

On September 13, after meeting with the president at the White House, Hillary told reporters she would support Bush "for a long time to come." The next day, when Bush visited Ground Zero and famously proclaimed, "I can hear you," Hillary cheered along with firefighters and police.

But that same crowd booed Hillary a week later when she appeared at Paul McCartney's Twin Towers relief concert. Firefighters and police jeered, "We don't want you here!" and

"Get off the stage!" In a bit of Soviet-style revisionism, the boos were replaced by cheers by the time the concert was aired on VH-1 and sold as a DVD.

Hillary's support for Bush was not just rhetorical. In October 2001, she voted for the Patriot Act, which gave authorities broad new powers in fighting terrorism. A year later, she voted for a resolution authorizing Bush to wage war against Iraq. She did this without reading the National Intelligence Estimate, the most detailed explanation of U.S. intelligence on weapons of mass destruction in Iraq. Although the classified, ninety-page report was made available to all senators ten days before the Iraq War vote, Hillary was one of ninety-four senators who chose not to read it. Nonetheless, she spoke with conviction about Saddam's arsenal.

"Intelligence reports show that Saddam Hussein has worked to rebuild his chemical and biological weapons stock, his missile delivery capability, and his nuclear program," Hillary said on the Senate floor. "He has also given aid, comfort, and sanctuary to terrorists, including al Qaeda members, though there is apparently no evidence of his involvement in the terrible events of September 11, 2001. It is clear, however, that if left unchecked, Saddam Hussein will continue to increase his capacity to wage biological and chemical warfare, and will keep trying to develop nuclear weapons.

"Should he succeed in that endeavor, he could alter the political and security landscape of the Middle East, which as we know all too well affects American security," she added. "This much is undisputed."

Her use of the word "undisputed" was significant. It signaled that Hillary was not placing the onus of proof on Bush. Indeed, she was determined to let the world know that she was making up her own mind, not blindly following the president. So she asserted without condition that "intelligence reports show" the gravity of the threat.

"Perhaps my decision is influenced by my eight years of experience on the other end of Pennsylvania Avenue in the White House, watching my husband deal with serious challenges to our nation," she explained.

Indeed, her husband had signed a 1998 law that made regime change in Iraq the official policy of the United States. Back then, Bill said of Saddam: "Mark my words, he will develop weapons of mass destruction. He will deploy them and he will use them."

Such rhetoric clearly had an impact on Hillary, who became more hawkish than most of her fellow Democrats when it came to giving Bush the authority to depose Saddam.

"We need a tough-minded, muscular foreign and defense policy," she said.

"This is probably the hardest decision I have ever had to make—any vote that may lead to war should be hard—but I cast it with conviction," she said. "It is with conviction that I support this resolution as being in the best interests of our nation."

Indeed, Hillary had so much conviction that she voted against an amendment that would have required Bush to come back to Congress for a second, more explicit authorization in the event that the United Nations balked at war.

Operation Iraqi Freedom, which began in March 2003, succeeded in liberating Iraq from Saddam's brutal dictatorship in a matter of weeks. But the U.S.-led coalition misjudged the tenacity of a post-Saddam insurgency, which grew bloodier with each passing month. Still, Hillary stood by her vote.

"I was one who supported giving President Bush the authority, if necessary, to use force against Saddam Hussein," she said in a December 2003 speech. "I believe that that was the right vote. I have had many disputes and disagreements with the administration over how that authority has been used.

"But I stand by the vote to provide the authority because I think it was a necessary step in order to maximize the outcome," she added. "And I also knew that our military forces would be successful."

When she spoke of her commitment to the war, Hillary sounded a lot like Bush.

"We have no option but to stay involved and committed," she said. "We need more of something that is often in short supply here in our country: patience."

How much patience? Hillary pointed to Germany, where U.S. forces have been stationed since the end of World War II.

"It took ten years to create a stable, sovereign government, and we still have troops in Germany, as we do in Japan, as we do in South Korea, as we do in Bosnia, as we do in Kosovo," she said. "So the idea that we can somehow bring about dramatic transformational change in either a short period of time or with a relatively limited financial commitment is contradicted by our own history. And therefore we have not only the need for patience, but a sense that we are going to be involved over the long run, or we will not guarantee or create the conditions for potential success."

Hillary said it was imperative "to maintain domestic support for the patience that is required and the commitment that we've undertaken, since failure is not an option."

"I worry a lot about how difficult it will be in the political arena to stay the course," she fretted. "To create a deep and lasting support for what is necessary to be done to protect ourselves and to spread our values around the world, over however many years it may take."

Again, her choice of words was important. It was difficult to imagine a more open-ended formulation than "however many years it may take."

Fourteen months later, with the United States still struggling to contain the insurgency, Hillary refused to join fellow Democrats in demanding a specific timetable for withdrawing troops.

"At this point in time, I think that would be a mistake," she told NBC in February 2005. "We don't want to send a signal to the insurgents, to the terrorists that we are going to be out of here at some, you know, date certain. I think that would be like a green light to go ahead and just bide your time."

"It is not in anyone's interests," she added, "for the Iraqi government to be brought down before it even can get itself together by violent insurgents."

NEVER HAVING TO SAY SHE'S SORRY

Nine months later, former North Carolina senator John Edwards, who had voted along with Hillary to authorize the war, published an op-ed column in the *Washington Post* that began, "I was wrong." Edwards, who was seeking the Democratic presidential nomination, was moving to the left and figured the only way to win over liberals was to repudiate his vote. But Hillary, who was already plotting her own White House bid, could not bring herself to utter such a mea culpa.

"Her reticence to admit a mistake," wrote Gerth and Van Natta, "lies in part in her own idealized view of herself, that she can do no wrong, as long as whatever mistake she made was in the pursuit of a larger good cause.

"Along with that comes the confidence that in any room she enters, she is the smartest," they added. "When good things happened, they happened because of Bill and Hillary. When bad things happened, Hillary often found the fault in others."

In the case of her vote for the Iraq War, Hillary began to shift the blame toward Bush.

"I do not think it is a smart strategy either for the president to continue with his open-ended commitment, which I think does not put enough pressure on the new Iraqi government, nor do I think it is smart strategy to set a date certain," she told an audience of booing and hissing liberals at the Take Back America conference in June 2006.

Hillary was trying to have it both ways. She was claiming to oppose both an open-ended commitment and a timetable. But the only way to terminate an open-ended commitment was to set a timetable.

A week later, during a speech on the Senate floor, Hillary heaped even more blame on the president.

"The Bush administration misused the authority granted to it," she said, "all the while viewing the dangerous and unstable conditions in Iraq through rose-colored glasses and the prism of electoral politics here at home."

But Hillary was looking through her own prism of electoral politics as she prepared for a White House bid. She was coming under intense pressure from the increasingly powerful liberal wing of the Democratic Party to abandon her opposition to a timetable.

"I've taken a lot of heat from my friends who have said, 'Please, just throw in the towel and say let's get out by a date certain,' " she told ABC in September 2006. "I don't think that's responsible."

But resisting a timetable carried a heavy political price for Hillary. Before long, the strain began to show.

"Everything I do carries political risk because nobody gets the scrutiny that I get," she complained to *Atlantic* magazine. "It's not like I have any margin for error whatsoever. I don't. Everybody else does, and I don't. And that's fine. That's just who I am, and that's what I live with."

Hillary seemed particularly bothered by rival Democrats who scored easy points with liberal activists by unequivocally repudiating the Iraq war.

"I am cursed with the responsibility gene," she lamented to the *New York Times*. "I am. I admit to that. You've got to be very careful in how you proceed with any combat situation in which American lives are at stake."

Feeling a bit sorry for herself, she confided to *New Yorker* magazine: "You know, I find myself, as I often do, in the somewhat lonely middle."

In December 2006, shortly after winning re-election to the Senate, Hillary was asked for the umpteenth time to defend her Iraq War vote.

"If we knew then what we know now, there wouldn't have been a vote," she told NBC. "And I certainly wouldn't have voted that way."

It had taken three years, but Hillary had now completely reversed course. Back in December 2003, when it was clear that Iraq had no weapons of mass destruction and that Bush had misjudged the insurgency, Hillary nonetheless declared: "I stand by the vote." But in December 2006, when she was about to formally declare her presidential candidacy, she said: "I certainly wouldn't have voted that way."

Hillary would make an even more dramatic about-face just weeks later. On January 17, she reiterated to the *New York Times* her opposition to a timetable.

"I am not for imposing a date-certain withdrawal date," she said.

But sixteen days later, during the Democratic National Committee's winter meeting in Washington, Hillary embraced a date certain after all.

"If we in Congress don't end this war before January of 2009, as president I will," she vowed.

This two-year deadline for withdrawing troops from Iraq

was directly at odds with Hillary's long-standing opposition to a specific timetable. It also contradicted her December 2003 assertion that the United States needed to "stay the course" in the struggle against terrorism, "however many years it may take."

Instead of acquiescing to Democratic demands for a withdrawal, Bush announced plans to "surge" more than twenty thousand additional troops into Iraq in an effort to bring sectarian violence under control. Hillary immediately pronounced this "a losing strategy." Having abandoned her call to "stay the course," she now proposed "a change of course, not adding more troops pursuing a strategy that, under present circumstances, cannot be successful." She demanded a cap on the number of troops at 130,000, the level at the start of 2007.

This did not satisfy many liberals, who continued to demand that Hillary explicitly repudiate her Iraq War vote, as John Edwards had done. One such demand came from a financial adviser named Roger Tilton at a town hall meeting in New Hampshire in February 2007.

"I want to know if—right here, right now, once and for all and without nuance—you can say that war authorization was a mistake," Tilton told Hillary. "I, and I think a lot of other primary voters—until we hear you say it, we're not going to hear all the other great things you are saying."

"Well, I have said, and I will repeat it, that knowing what I know now, I never would have voted for it," Hillary said. "But I also, I mean, obviously you have to weigh everything as you make your decision. I have taken responsibility for my vote. The mistakes were made by this president, who misled this country and this Congress into a war that should not have been waged."

Hillary had now shifted all blame for the Iraq War onto Bush. Never mind that she had once said it was "undisputed" that "if left unchecked, Saddam Hussein will continue to increase his capacity to wage biological and chemical warfare, and will keep trying to develop nuclear weapons."

A week after her encounter with Roger Tilton, Hillary again found herself again in New Hampshire, again defending her Iraq War vote.

"If the most important thing to any of you is choosing someone who did not cast that vote or has said his vote was a mistake, then there are others to choose from," she said.

It was reminiscent of her Tammy Wynette moment, fifteen years earlier, when she snapped that if voters had a problem with her husband's adultery, "then heck, don't vote for him."

The same day that Hillary invited New Hampshire voters to choose another Democratic presidential candidate, she gave an interview to the *New York Times* that underscored just how profoundly she had changed her tune on Iraq.

"Look, I think the American people are done with Iraq," she said. "I think they are at a point where, whether they thought it was a good idea or not, they have seen misjudgment and blunder after blunder, and their attitude is: What is this getting us? What is this doing for us?"

"No one wants to sit by and see mass killing," she added. "It's going on every day! Thousands of people are dying every month in Iraq. Our presence there is not stopping it. And there is no potential opportunity I can imagine where it could. This is an Iraqi problem; we cannot save the Iraqis from themselves."

Gone was the perseverance that Hillary had espoused back in December 2003, when she reminded Americans that it took postwar Germany a decade to find its footing. Gone was the pluck that Hillary had personified when she rallied for "something that is often in short supply here in our country: patience."

Hillary went on to tell the *Times* that Bush should begin withdrawing troops instead of pursuing the surge, which she said had little chance of success.

"I think it's more likely that the anti-American violence and sectarian violence just moves from place to place to place, like the old Whac-A-Mole," she said. "Clear some neighborhoods in Baghdad, then face Ramadi. Clear Ramadi, then maybe it's back in Falluja."

But the opposite happened. Soldiers cleared neighborhoods and then stayed there to prevent terrorists from returning. As the months passed and violence dropped, even some Democrats began to acknowledge the surge was working. Senate Majority Whip Dick Durbin, who initially opposed the surge, told reporters after a visit to Iraq in August that surge troops were "starting to have an impact" by "making real progress" in "routing out the al Qaeda."

A turning point in the conventional wisdom occurred when Democratic scholars Michael O'Hanlon and Kenneth Pollack of the liberal Brookings Institution wrote an op-ed column in the *New York Times* headlined "A War We Just Might Win."

"We are finally getting somewhere in Iraq," they concluded after visiting Iraq. "We were surprised by the gains we saw."

By now, Hillary had shortened her withdrawal timetable from January 2009 to March 2008, as proposed in a Democratic Senate resolution. Still haunted by her original Iraq War vote, she kept searching for a way to take it back. Of course, this was impossible, but she eventually came up with the next best thing. She called on Congress to "deauthorize" the war on October 11, 2007, the fifth anniversary of its authorization.

"I'M YOUR GIRL!"

On January 16, 2007, freshman senator Barack Obama of Illinois announced that he was filing papers to become a candidate for the Democratic presidential nomination. The announcement drew massive media coverage. Reporters hailed Obama as the first African-American to have a realistic shot at capturing the White House. They pointed out that Obama, unlike Hillary, had publicly opposed the Iraq War from the very beginning. Determined to cut short this lovefest, Hillary spent the next day recording her own presidential campaign announcement at her Washington mansion. Mindful of her image as cold and unapproachable, she looked directly into the camera and tried to project an informal, friendly image. Three days later, she posted the video on the internet under the heading, "I'm in and I'm in to win."

"Let's talk. Let's chat. Let's start a dialogue about your ideas and mine," she said with a smile. "Because the conversation in

Washington has been just a little one-sided lately, don't you think? And we can all see how well that works."

The announcement succeeded in choking off the media oxygen to Obama's fledgling campaign. But Hillary could not keep him down for long. Obama quickly began picking off big Democratic donors who had previously been loyal to Team Clinton. One of the biggest was Hollywood producer David Geffen, who had raised $18 million for Bill Clinton, earning himself a night in the Lincoln Bedroom. But now Geffen was raising money for Obama. Adding insult to injury, he trashed Hillary in an interview with *New York Times* columnist Maureen Dowd.

"I don't think that another incredibly polarizing figure, no matter how smart she is and no matter how ambitious she is —and God knows, is there anybody more ambitious than Hillary Clinton?—can bring the country together," Geffen railed. "It's not a very big thing to say 'I made a mistake' on the war, and typical of Hillary Clinton that she can't."

Geffen said he hoped Obama could stand up to what Dowd called "Clinton Inc."

"That machine is going to be very unpleasant and unattractive and effective," he said of Hillary's campaign.

"She's so advised by so many smart advisers who are covering every base," he added. "I think that America was better served when the candidates were chosen in smoke-filled rooms."

He concluded that "the Clintons were unwilling to stand for the things that they genuinely believe in. Everybody in politics lies, but they do it with such ease, it's troubling."

The blunt remarks so rattled Hillary that she instructed her campaign to lash out at Obama, which merely served to give the story legs. Pundits clucked that Hillary should have let the story die by ignoring it. But the battle-hardened candidate disagreed.

"I've learned a lot of lessons being involved in politics," she told a crowd in Iowa. "I also believe that when you are attacked, you have to deck your opponents."

But Obama was proving difficult to deck. In fact, Americans were mesmerized by an underground campaign ad that urged voters to support Obama over Hillary. The internet ad was an adaptation of the iconic "1984" television spot that had introduced Apple Macintosh computers twenty-three years earlier. Images of Hillary were substituted for the Orwellian "Big Brother" in the original spot. In the updated version, row after row of mind-numbed "proles" stare vacantly at a giant screen of Hillary dispensing banalities. Then a colorfully dressed woman, chased by storm troopers, hurls a sledgehammer that shatters the screen and frees the proles from their oppression. The "viral" video, entitled "Vote Different," was viewed more than a million times on the popular website YouTube and replayed endlessly on TV news broadcasts. It underscored Obama's image as the fresh face in the campaign.

Hillary tried valiantly to freshen up her own image on the campaign trail, with mixed results. For example, when addressing audiences, she sometimes made the mistake of following her husband. This only served to highlight Bill's considerable oratorical gifts, while making Hillary sound flat and uninspiring by comparison. When she allowed herself to wax lyrical at a Baptist church in Selma, Alabama, she was accused of faking a southern accent.

But these were minor flaps compared to the central challenge of Hillary's campaign—shedding the "baggage" known as the legendary Clinton scandals. That's the way it was described by the *New York Times* in a front-page article that raised questions about the Clintons' marriage and hinted darkly that Bill might still be cheating on Hillary.

"Mr. Clinton is rarely without company in public, yet the company he keeps rarely includes his wife," insinuated *Times* reporter Patrick Healy in 2006. "Nights out find him zipping around Los Angeles with his bachelor buddy, Ronald W. Burkle, or hitting parties and fund-raisers in Manhattan; she is yoked to work in Washington or New York—her Senate career and political ambitions consuming her time."

The story reported that "since leaving the White House, Bill and Hillary Clinton have built largely separate lives." The article went on to suggest that would-be supporters of Hillary might be "distracted" by the fact that her husband had an affair with White House intern Monica Lewinsky. Hillary's presidential campaign, the story said, could stir up memories of "the soap opera of infidelity." Even Democratic supporters like Lanny Davis, who worked for Bill in the White House, fretted that the former president's relationship with Hillary "might hurt her—all those old memories and scandals will be evoked."

"Because of Mr. Clinton's behavior in the White House, tabloid gossip sticks to him like iron filings to a magnet," Healy wrote. "Several prominent New York Democrats, in interviews, volunteered that they became concerned last year over a tabloid photograph showing Mr. Clinton leaving B.L.T. Steak in Midtown Manhattan late one night after dining with a group that included Belinda Stronach, a Canadian politician. The two were among roughly a dozen people at a dinner, but it still was enough to fuel coverage in the gossip pages."

And in the vaunted *New York Times*.

Hillary insists her battle scars from the scandal wars are actually a positive, not a negative, in the 2008 presidential race.

"For fifteen years I have stood up against the right-wing machine, and I've come out stronger," she said at a Democratic debate in August 2007. "So if you want a winner who knows how to take them on, I'm your girl!"

WHERE HILLARY CLINTON STANDS ON THE ISSUES

ABORTION
Pro-choice, but adds: "Abortion in many ways represents a sad, even tragic choice to many, many women."

CLIMATE CHANGE
"We are causing the planet to warm, with potentially devastating consequences." Favors mandatory cuts in emissions.

GAY MARRIAGE

Opposes gay marriage, but also opposes a constitutional ban on gay marriage.

HEALTH CARE

Favors a revamped plan for national health care after failing to implement earlier version as First Lady.

IMMIGRATION

Supports President Bush's call for a guest worker program that would grant legal status to illegal aliens.

IRAQ

Initially voted for the war and opposed both a withdrawal timetable and funding cut-off. Now opposes war and supports both a withdrawal timetable and funding cut-off.

TAXES

Wants to raise taxes on upper-income earners.

3

RUDY GIULIANI

"I've led a very complex life," Rudy Giuliani told me with a chuckle in perhaps the biggest understatement of the 2008 presidential campaign.

Indeed, "complex" does not begin to capture the operatic personal life of Rudolph William Giuliani. His first wife was his second cousin. His second wife stayed in the mayor's official residence, Gracie Mansion, while Giuliani moved in with two gay men and began dating a woman who would become his third wife (who has also been married three times). His relationship with his children (from his second wife) is so strained that his daughter is supporting rival presidential candidate Barack Obama. Got all that?

On the other hand, there is no denying Giuliani's remarkable achievements. Rejecting the criminal life of his own father, a felon who served time at Sing Sing, Giuliani grew up to become the most celebrated prosecutor in America. Later, as mayor of New York, he transformed a crime-infested cesspool into a family-friendly tourist destination. And his unflinching leadership in response to the terrorist attacks of September 11 elevated him to the heroic status of "America's Mayor." His popularity even transcends his deep disagreements with fellow Republicans over potent social issues such as abortion and gun control. If he can manage to keep enough of those conservatives from bolting, Rudy Giuliani might very well become the next president.

UNORTHODOX ORIGINS

Harold Giuliani served time in Sing Sing for robbing a milkman a decade before the birth of his only child, Rudy. The unemployed plumber's assistant pulled a gun on his victim in a Manhattan apartment building and was in the process of tying him up when a policeman walked in and arrested the twenty-six-year-old thief. After lying to authorities about his name, age, and address, Harold eventually came clean and spent more than a year in the legendary maximum-security prison. He was paroled in 1935 and resumed his courtship of Helen D'Avanzo, whom he had been dating since 1930. The two, whose parents had emigrated from Italy in the late 1800s, were married in 1936. Eight years later, Helen gave birth to Rudy. The family lived with Helen's mother, Adelino, in the upstairs apartment of a duplex in the East Flatbush neighborhood of Brooklyn.

Harold, whose felony conviction precluded him from serving in the military during World War II, eventually became a bartender at Vincent's Restaurant, which was owned by a relative. According to *Rudy!,* an exhaustive biography by *Village Voice* reporter Wayne Barrett, the future presidential candidate's father moonlighted as a violent enforcer for a loansharking operation. The book, which also revealed Harold's stint at Sing Sing, came as something of a "shock" to Rudy, he acknowledged a month after its release in 2000.

"Some of it I knew, some of it I suspected, some of it I absolutely didn't know," he told NY1 television. "When I write my book, I'll explain which is which."

Rudy said his decision to go into law enforcement may have been driven in part by Harold's checkered past. In fact, he described his conscience-stricken father as "compulsive about being honest."

"He would tell me, 'Never take anybody else's money, make sure you always pay for things, make sure that you don't make a mistake when you fill out a form, make sure it's accurate,' " he told NY1. "I've driven myself crazy over this all my life. And when any mistake has been made it really bothers me, and I realize more than I did as I was growing up why my father was doing that. I mean, he wanted to make sure that I didn't make the same mistakes that he believed he had made."

To prevent young Rudy from ending up like some of his cousins, who were linked to organized crime, his family left Brooklyn in 1951 and moved to suburban Nassau County on Long Island.

"I think the decision that my father and mother made, essentially, was to take me out of Brooklyn, where they thought

I could get into trouble," Giuliani said, "and keep me away from some of the things that I guess my father was worried about."

Looking back on his father's life, Giuliani was philosophical during an interview with the *New York Times*.

"My father wasn't terribly successful, but he had no bitterness," he said, adding that the old man's unfulfilled ambition "was sort of pushed into me."

In 1957, Giuliani began commuting to Brooklyn to attend Bishop Loughlin Memorial High, a Roman Catholic school for boys, where he entertained the possibility of becoming a priest. He also started an opera club and was listed as "Class Politician" in his senior yearbook. An avid admirer of John F. Kennedy, Giuliani managed to meet the president his senior year and even portrayed him at a mock political convention put on by the school.

After graduation, Giuliani enrolled in Manhattan College, an all-male, Roman Catholic school in the Bronx. In 1961, as President Kennedy was sending thirteen hundred advisers to South Vietnam, Giuliani joined the Air Force ROTC. He would remain in the program for two years, leaving in 1963, just as American involvement in Vietnam started to escalate.

"I got washed out of flight training because when I was young, I punctured two eardrums," Giuliani explained to *New York* magazine. "It caused a minor hearing problem. I was very disappointed because I wanted to fly."

Meanwhile, he had been bitten by the political bug. He won an election for president of his sophomore class at Manhattan, only to lose the next year's contest. He also became president of his fraternity and began writing a regular column for the student newspaper, the *Quadrangle*. In 1964, he wrote about Attorney General Robert F. Kennedy, whose aggressive prosecution of the Teamsters had fascinated Giuliani. Kennedy was now running for the U.S. Senate seat in New York and coming under attack because he had never lived in the state. Giuliani rode to his hero's defense in a column that would resurface decades later, when he mounted his own Senate bid against Hillary Rodham Clinton, who also had never lived in New York.

"The 'carpetbagger' issue," Giuliani wrote, "is a truly ridiculous reason for not voting for a man in the year 1964. Without doubt, the Kennedy candidacy in New York is perfectly in accord with the Constitutional stipulation that a senator must be a resident of the state he represents on the day he is elected."

Giuliani added: "Let us hope that cosmopolitan New Yorkers can rise above the ridiculous, time-worn provincial attitude that has so disunified our nation. A Kennedy victory will bring about the assertion of a most valuable precedent; that a representative from a particular state must be able to think and vote in the light of national needs and not to be tied only to local and sectional pressures."

After graduating from Manhattan in 1965 with a political science degree (and a philosophy minor), Giuliani enrolled at New York University Law School, where he made law review his freshman year. He also concluded, after years of soul-searching, that he would never become a priest.

"The priesthood is a vocation," he told the *Times*. "And I probably didn't have it. I probably just thought I had it."

Still, Catholicism would remain an integral part of Giuliani's life.

"My faith is part of my development, it's part of my thinking, it's part of how I look at the world, how I look at life," he told me. "Until I was twenty-three or twenty-four years old, I never started a class without saying a prayer."

Over the following decades, Giuliani's fascination with faith only deepened.

"I have tremendous interest in religion," he told me. "I can sit down and discuss with you the history of the Anglican religion, the Methodist religion, Wesley, Knox, the whole Protestant Reformation, Greek Orthodox religion, Jewish Hasidim, where they came from—I love religion. I also believe, beyond just a state point of view, to understand human beings, you have to understand religion."

That's because Giuliani considers religion one the "core" human imperatives.

"You know, it's like understanding the need to eat to survive; it's like understanding the sexual drive," he told me. "The desire for God every human being has built into them somewhere because we're intelligent. Intellectually, they want an explanation of what this is all about. It doesn't make sense to them unless there's an explanation for it.

"So a lot of what I believe about democracy comes from my religion—and about humanism. But I feel the freedom to disagree with my religion when my conscience doesn't lead me to the same conclusion.

"And I understand that isn't the view that a lot of other people have of the religion they belong to. They believe that if you disagree, you have to submit to the authority of the religion. From my point of view, maybe my religion's a more personal religion, rather than an organized religion."

SCALING THE HEIGHTS OF POWER

Upon graduation from Manhattan College in the spring of 1968, Giuliani proposed to Regina Peruggi, whom he had known all his life. That's because they were second cousins (their fathers were first cousins). Normally, such an unusual union would require dispensation from the Catholic Church. But Rudy and Regina kept quiet about their common ancestry and were married that October in a Catholic ceremony in the Bronx.

"I was under the impression that we were third cousins because I never calculated the lines of consanguinity," Giuliani later explained to the *Times*. "I can't tell you what Gina thought. I don't think we ever discussed it in any great detail."

Meanwhile, Giuliani landed a job as a law clerk for U.S. District Judge Lloyd MacMahon, the top judge in the Southern District of New York. MacMahon would become an important mentor to the aspiring lawyer. The judge even wrote a letter to the local draft board, asking that his twenty-four-year-old clerk be granted an occupational deferment from the military draft during the height of the Vietnam War, which Giuliani opposed. The board, which had previously denied Giuliani's appeals, relented after being lobbied by the federal judge.

But the deferment expired in 1970, and Giuliani found himself again facing the prospect of being drafted. It is not clear whether his hearing problem from seven years earlier had persisted.

"I had student deferments during school, and then when I entered the draft lottery, I pulled number 300, 306, something like that," he told *New York* magazine.

The number was actually 308, considered high enough to guarantee that Giuliani would not be sent to Vietnam. But he said he would have gone if he had pulled a lower number.

"Oh sure, if I had to, even though I disagreed with it," he told the magazine. "I would have gone because it was my duty to go."

Three months after pulling his high draft number, Giuliani was sworn in as an assistant U.S. attorney in the Southern District. Over the next five years, the ambitious prosecutor rose through the ranks and eventually headed both the narcotics and corruption divisions. A registered Democrat, Giuliani voted for liberal George McGovern in the presidential election of 1972.

But he had soured on the Democratic Party by 1975, the year he moved to Washington to accept the job of associate deputy attorney general in President Gerald Ford's administration. So Giuliani changed his voter affiliation to independent. After Ford lost the election eighteen months later, the lawyer returned to New York and went to work for a private law firm, Patterson, Belknap, Webb and Tyler. When Ronald Reagan returned the White House to Republican hands in 1981, the thirty-six-year-old Giuliani returned to Washington to become the youngest ever associate attorney general, the number-three man at Justice. By now, he was also a registered Republican.

"I came to think that McGovern and the Democrats had a dangerous view," he later told the *Times*. "By the time I moved to Washington, the Republicans had come to make more sense to me."

Giuliani's meteoric rise through the legal profession came with a heavy price. His marriage was falling apart. In fact, Regina did not accompany Rudy to Washington this time around because they had separated in February 1980. They divorced in October 1982, by which time Giuliani was already engaged to his live-in girlfriend, TV broadcaster Donna Hanover. The soap-opera lifestyle raised eyebrows at the Justice Department, according to *Wall Street Journal* writer James B. Stewart, who chronicled Giuliani in his book *The Prosecutors*.

"His personal life," Stewart wrote, "caused acute discomfort in the upper ranks of the department, where rectitude was the order of the day. Giuliani had divorced his wife shortly after being appointed. Then he had begun dating his secretary in the department, a subject of much gossip. He was now engaged to a television personality. By contemporary standards, it was pretty innocuous stuff. But it deepened the gulf between him and his more staid superiors."

Giuliani needed to have his first marriage to his second cousin annulled so that he could wed Hanover in a Catholic church. He went to see an old friend, Alan Placa, a priest who had been best man at Rudy's wedding to Regina.

"You were related, you must have gotten a dispensation," Placa said, according to Giuliani's account to the *Times*.

"Alan, I don't recall doing that," Giuliani replied. "I don't recall realizing that I had to get one."

"Well, you know, the priest may have gone ahead and done it anyway," Placa replied.

The annulment was eventually granted, thereby ending a fourteen-year marriage that the Catholic Church probably would not have sanctioned if it had known the common ancestry of the bride and groom.

"We were second cousins," Giuliani told *New York* magazine. "We'd never gotten the proper dispensation when we got married. So under church rules, we were able to get it annulled."

The following year, Giuliani and Hanover left Washington and moved to New York so that Rudy could become U.S. attorney for the Southern District. He was now the top prosecutor in the office he had joined more than a dozen years earlier as a freshly minted lawyer.

In April 1984, Placa presided over the marriage of Giuliani and Hanover. A year later, the couple had their first child, Andrew, who was joined four years later by a sister, Caroline.

During this period, Giuliani sealed his reputation as a hard-charging prosecutor with a flair for making headlines.

"He presided over a stunning series of dramatic and daring prosecutions—mob and otherwise—that were the stuff of legend, even without a publicist," wrote Barrett in *Rudy!* "The media fed his burgeoning reputation—and he fed them with a regular regimen of juicy press conferences. He became a celebrity, a folk hero who, although unabashedly overzealous, even evangelical, earned apt comparisons to Eliot Ness."

One of Giuliani's highest-profile cases was the mafia "commission" case, in which he indicted eleven mob figures, including the heads of the five organized crime families dominating the East Coast. Vowing to "wipe out the five families," Giuliani secured convictions against mobsters such as "Fat Tony" Salerno and "Big Paul" Castellano. The prison sentences added up to hundreds of years.

Giuliani then turned his attention to white-collar crime, winning convictions against Wall Street financiers Ivan Boesky and Michael Milken for insider trading. The son of a convicted felon was now the most feared prosecutor in America. He was determined to parlay this reputation into a successful political career.

In 1989, Giuliani resigned from the attorney's office and announced his intention to run for mayor of New York City. He won the Republican primary, advancing to the general election in a face-off against David Dinkins, who had bested incumbent mayor Ed Koch in the Democratic primary. Giuliani argued in a debate with Dinkins that the Democrat, if elected, would amount to "more of the same, more of the rotten politics that have been dragging us down."

"If we keep going merrily along, this city's going down," Giuliani warned.

Dinkins countered that the city needed "a mayor, not a prosecutor," prompting Giuliani to fire back that New York wanted "a mayor who has nothing to fear from a prosecutor."

In the end, Dinkins won the election by a whisker. Giuliani returned to private practice for the first time in nearly a decade, where he bided his time for a rematch.

As part of his preparation, Giuliani commissioned two opposition researchers, Christopher Lyon and Ronald Giller, to compile an exhaustive "vulnerability study" on himself so that he could formulate responses to expected attacks. The massive, 450-page report was completed in April 1993.

"This study is tough and hard-hitting," the authors wrote. "It pulls no punches. It is not intended to shock or offend, but to prepare the candidate and his staff for the kind of no-holds-barred assault they should expect."

They added: "Taken together, the negative issues presented in this study offer a compelling argument against electing Giuliani mayor."

The authors were particularly worried about their client's reputation as a "draft dodger." Adopting the likely attack line of Giuliani's detractors, they wrote that he "received special treatment from a friendly federal judge to avoid military service during the Vietnam war, when thousands of less fortunate people were dying. Then, as a member of the Justice Department, he hypocritically prosecuted draft-dodgers."

To defend against this expected attack, the authors urged the campaign to counter: "Giuliani did not avoid military service. In fact, he joined the Air Force ROTC program, but was processed out because of an ear problem."

Rudy was also deemed vulnerable on his evolution from Democrat to Republican, which the authors of the study called a "flip-flop."

"Giuliani is a man without conviction," wrote Lyon and Giller, adopting the perspective of expected critics. "His political opportunism drove him from McGovern Democrat to Reagan Republican. He will do . . . anything it takes to get what he wants."

The authors urged campaign officials to deflect such attacks with creative spin about Giuliani being "the perfect non-politician politician. A man above party labels."

Finally, the report delved into Giuliani's fourteen-year marriage to his second cousin, saying it "raises questions about a 'weirdness factor.' " The authors said the marriage "has been raised in the media as an extremely bizarre event."

Lyon and Giller recommended that "Giuliani refuse to discuss this issue out of respect for Regina's privacy and because it is highly personal and has already been discussed at great length in the media."

In the end, Dinkins never raised the marriage issue. In fact, Giuliani was portrayed as hopelessly old-fashioned by the *New York Times* magazine, which labeled him "a Wonder Bread son of the '50s." The liberal publication archly observed: "It's as if his cultural and psychic sensibilities froze about 1961, the year he left the tutelage of the Christian Brothers at Bishop Loughlin."

On November 2, 1993, Republican challenger Rudy Giuliani unseated Democratic incumbent David Dinkins in the overwhelmingly liberal city, which was no mean feat. The Big Apple would never be quite the same.

POLISHING THE BIG APPLE

Employing the hard-charging style that had made him a celebrity prosecutor, Giuliani set about wresting control of the city away from the criminals, smut peddlers, panhandlers, and vagrants who had turned New York into a dangerous and forbidding place. Beefing up the police force, Giuliani slashed crime, cleaned up Times Square, and generally made New York much safer, cleaner, and more hospitable. The remarkable transformation delighted tourists and impressed even jaded locals.

"We went from crime capital to safest large city in America," Giuliani told me. "I ended up reducing crime five times more than anybody thought."

But crime was only one of many social ills that Giuliani set out to cure.

"We went from welfare capital to the welfare-to-work capital—640,000 fewer people on welfare," he boasted. "We went from a city that had double-digit unemployment to a city that had half that."

He added: "We also went from a city that was hopeless to a city that was very optimistic. We went from a city where people wanted to leave, to a city people wanted to come to—and stay. And I think those are real achievements."

But critics said Giuliani's police force went too far, especially in pursuit of minorities. In 1997, a black immigrant from Haiti named Abner Louima was sodomized with a broom handle by police officers in Brooklyn. Giuliani denounced Louima's attackers, who were convicted and imprisoned amid public demonstrations against police brutality.

Two years later, however, Giuliani fiercely defended four plainclothes officers who fired forty-one bullets into an unarmed black immigrant from Africa named Amadou Diallo. Again, there were cries of police brutality, although this time the cops were cleared of wrongdoing.

The mayor easily won re-election in 1997, although he was prohibited by law from seeking a third term. So in April 1999, he formed an exploratory committee to run for the U.S. Senate seat being vacated by Daniel Patrick Moynihan. First Lady Hillary Rodham Clinton was also eyeing the seat, setting up a potential clash of political titans.

But on April 26, 2000, Giuliani was diagnosed with prostate cancer, a disease that had claimed his father's life nineteen years earlier. The mayor made the news public the next day at a press conference.

"Are there any circumstances under which you would drop from the Senate race?" a reporter asked.

"I don't think it's fair to answer questions about the Senate race right now," Giuliani replied. "I think that my focus right now has to be on how to figure out the best form of treatment, and then after I decide that, and get a while to absorb this, to figure out, you know, should I do it? Would I be able to do it the right way? I hope that's the case."

A few days after the announcement, New York's tabloids published photos of Giuliani dining in public with Judith Nathan, forty-five, a twice-divorced sales manager for a pharmaceutical firm. The city's press corps went into a feeding frenzy.

"She's a good friend, a very good friend," Giuliani allowed.

Truth be told, Giuliani's second marriage had been on the rocks for years. In 1997, *Vanity Fair* published an article that all but accused the mayor of having an affair with his communications director, Cristyne Lategano. By the spring of 1999, Giuliani quietly began seeing Nathan, even though he was still living with his wife, Hanover, and their two children, in the mayor's residence, Gracie Mansion.

Days after his affair with Nathan went public, a visibly shaken Giuliani abruptly called a press conference to announce that he wanted a separation from Hanover.

"This is very, very painful," Giuliani told reporters. "For quite some time it's probably been apparent that Donna and I lead, in many ways, independent and separate lives."

He added: "I am hopeful that we will be able to formalize that in an agreement that protects our children, gives them the security and all the protection they deserve, and protects Donna."

Giuliani refused to say whether he would pull out of the Senate race.

"I don't really care about politics right now," he said. "I'm thinking about my family, the people that I love, and what can be done that's honest and truthful and that protects them the best."

But his bombshell announcement had blindsided Hanover, fifty, who responded with her own press conference three hours later.

"Today's turn of events brings me great sadness," the tearful wife said. "I had hoped to keep this marriage together. For several years it was difficult to participate in Rudy's public life because of his relationship with one staff member. Beginning last May, I made a major effort to bring us back together, and Rudy and I re-established some of our personal intimacy through the fall. At that point, he chose another path. Rudy and I will now discuss the possibility of a legal separation."

Nine days after these dueling press conferences, Giuliani dropped out of the Senate race. He said it was because of the cancer, not the extraordinary swirl of scandal surrounding his personal life.

"I've decided that what I should do is to put my health first," he said. "This is not the right time for me to run for office."

Speaking with an unusual degree of introspection, Giuliani said the cancer had changed his entire outlook.

"I used to think the core of me was in politics," he said. "I used to make many of my life decisions for the last ten years around politics. And they should have been made—and I'm going to make them in the future—around the other things."

Which "other things" did he mean?

"Your life is more important, your health is more important, the people you love, your family, people that are close to you and really care about you. You know, those are the most important things in life," he said. "I think I understand myself a lot better. I think I understand what's important."

Humbled by the disease and embarrassed by the failure of his second marriage, Giuliani said "something beautiful" had grown out of his anguish.

"You confront your limits, you confront your mortality, you realize that you're not a superman, that you're just a human being," he said.

He acknowledged being a polarizing figure to some New Yorkers, particularly minorities, and pledged to make amends during his remaining time in office by reaching out to "every New Yorker."

"I want to protect them," he said. "I believe this is the right decision. And I think somehow, somewhere, some way, this is all for the best. And it's going to mean that I can be a better mayor, and I'm going to try to use it for that."

"Mr. Mayor," a reporter said, "is this the end of your political career?"

"I don't think I'm thinking about politics," Giuliani replied. "I'm thinking about deeper, deeper things than that."

When another reporter asked whether he now felt "closer to God," Giuliani quipped, "I hope he's closer to me."

A few weeks later, Giuliani got the separation he sought, but Hanover got the house. Never mind that it was Gracie Mansion. The mayor moved out of his official residence and started living with two gay men in an apartment on the Upper East Side. He and Hanover began a protracted and nasty divorce battle. And the tabloids rejoiced at the embarrassment of riches.

FROM "BUM" TO "HERO"?

On the morning of September 11, 2001, Giuliani's security detail was notified that a small airplane, perhaps a Cessna, had crashed into the World Trade Center. Since the mayor made it his business to personally show up at the scene of crises in the city, he and his aides piled into a van and headed for the crash site.

"By bending down in the backseat, I could see the very top of the north tower. There were flames coming from the upper floors. At that distance, it looked bad but not unmanageable," he later wrote in his book, *Leadership*. "My first assumption was that it was some nut flying in a small plane."

But the gravity of the situation began to dawn on Giuliani when he passed St. Vincent's Hospital and saw doctors and nurses in operating gowns preparing for triage on the sidewalk.

"Then the second plane hit. All I saw was a big flash of fire," he recalled. "Initially, I thought it was the first tower experiencing a secondary explosion."

He added: "We continued rushing south toward the scene. Driving by, I could see the stunned expression on every face as people stared up at the nightmare unfolding before their eyes."

Upon arrival at the scene, Giuliani met Police Commissioner Bernard Kerik and went looking for the fire commander.

"I hurried down West Street, to the fire command post, and on the way there saw something that made me realize that we were in a new world," he wrote in *Leadership*. "I looked up and saw what I took to be debris falling from the building."

But then Giuliani took a closer look and realized that all of the city's carefully prepared emergency response plans would be utterly useless in a catastrophe of this magnitude.

"I focused on a man leaning out of a window of what must have been about the 102nd floor of Tower 1. I saw him jump and followed his whole trajectory as he plummeted onto the roof of 6 World Trade Center, the building just north of Tower 1. That someone would choose certain death brought home the reality of what was unfolding on the floors above where the planes had hit. I grabbed Bernie's arm and said, 'We're in uncharted waters now. We're going to have to make up our response.' I looked up again and saw other people jumping. Some appeared to be holding hands as they plummeted. They were not blown out of the building. They were making the conscious decision that it was better to die that way than to face the two-thousand-degree heat of the blazing jet fuel.''

Giuliani hurried on to the fire command post, where he encountered top fire officials such as Bill Feehan, Pete Gancy, and Ray Downey.

"Tell me what I should tell people," the mayor implored Gancy.

"To get out of the building," Gancy replied.

With chunks of that building raining down all around them, Giuliani told Gancy: "I think you should move this command post."

The mayor also needed to set up his own command post so that city government could function during the crisis. He couldn't use City Hall, which had been evacuated and sealed off. Nor could he use the site that had been designated for such emergencies, since it was in the World Trade Center. So Giuliani said good-bye to the cluster of fire officials, which by now included Father Mychal Judge, the department's chaplain, before continuing his search.

"I had known these men—Bill and Pete and Ray and Father Judge—for many years, had looked up to them and pinned medals on them," he later wrote. "I loved these men. I did not realize that this would be the last time I would ever see them. All four died that day."

During my interview with Giuliani, he elaborated on his devastation over Judge's death.

"The only other time in my life I had a similar feeling was when I lost my own father," he told me.

Before learning of Judge's death, Giuliani made a mental note to consult with the priest within a few hours.

"I knew before the end of the day, I was going to have to start explaining death again," he told me. "And he was always the person I'd go to, to help me do that, because we'd been at the bedsides of so many firefighters and police officers.

"And he also—when I had difficulties, in my marriage, when they were public—he would write me beautiful notes," Giuliani added. "He wouldn't let me off the hook completely. He would explain to me where I had sinned.

"But he would tell me also you've got to go back, you've got to go back to the full, complete life that you've led, and the things that you've done for people. And you've got to overcome some of these problems. But you've got to see it in the context that you're basically a good person. And also, never be embarrassed, no matter what you did. Jesus will always love you; he'll always be there for you."

Giuliani and his entourage commandeered an office building adjacent to the World Trade Center that had functioning phone lines. The mayor was patched through to Vice President Dick Cheney at the White House, but the line went dead as the conversation was about to begin. Just then, Giuliani said he "felt and heard a thunderous roar." Outside, one of the twin towers had collapsed, enveloping lower Manhattan in a gargantuan cloud of ash and smoke.

"Boss, we've got to get out of here," said a security official as he grabbed Giuliani's arm.

But enormous chunks of concrete and twisted steel now blocked all exits in the front of the building, which faced the disaster site to the south. And even if they had been able to get out that way, they would have emerged into the blindness of a toxic cloud so thick that it blotted out the sun. So the group headed north in search of an exit at the back of the building. But every door they tried—one on the first floor and three in the basement—was chained or locked tight. Finally, they were guided by a pair of janitors through a basement passageway that led them into the lobby of an adjacent building to the north. But even that was unsafe.

"All hell was breaking loose," Giuliani recalled. "The lobby was surrounded by windows, and all we could see was an impenetrable cloud of white—we couldn't make out anything beyond the glass. Stuff was blowing through the streets like the tornado scene from *The Wizard of Oz.*"

Giuliani's growing band of stragglers now included people who were caked in white ash and spattered with blood.

"We stayed there for a couple of minutes, then I made the decision to move out," he recalled. "If we were inside and the building collapsed, a big portion of city government would be eliminated. Outside, there was a better chance that we could re-establish city government. I had a fleeting thought that I'd rather be hurt on the street than crushed within the building, but I had to put that thought out of my mind. I had to focus on finding the press and communicating with people to give them advice."

Giuliani emerged from the building and began a walking press conference. He got four blocks north of the World Trade Center before the second tower fell.

"It was primitive, shocking, surreal," Giuliani recalled. "And above the dust and soot and glass that still rained down was the same perfect blue sky."

The mayor continued north for a few blocks until he reached an empty firehouse, where one of his aides jimmied open a locked door. Giuliani got on the telephone to NY1 TV and urged residents to remain calm as they evacuated lower Manhattan. Noting that he had already been in touch with the White House, the mayor assured New Yorkers that the city was being protected by military jets.

"My heart goes out to all of you," he said. "I've never seen anything like this. I was there shortly after it happened and saw people jumping out of the World Trade Center. It's a horrible, horrible situation and all that I can tell you is that every resource that we have is attempting to rescue as many people as possible. The end result is going to be some horrendous number of lives lost. I don't think we know yet, but right now we have to focus on saving as many people as possible."

As the day wore on, Giuliani tried to reassure the shell-shocked public.

"Tomorrow, New York is going to be here," he said. "And we're going to rebuild, and we're going to be stronger than we were before."

He added: "I want the people of New York to be an example to the rest of the country, and the rest of the world, that terrorism can't stop us."

Time magazine would later observe that "Giuliani became the voice of America. Every time he spoke, millions of people felt a little better. His words were full of grief and iron, inspiring New York to inspire the nation."

The mayor went to Ground Zero at least half a dozen times on September 11. The last time was late at night, when rescue workers were digging through the rubble under banks of enormous lights. Giuliani recounted the scene in *Leadership*.

"Several times, I closed my eyes and expected to open them and see the twin towers still standing. *This is not real. This is not real. This is not real.* Then I'd shake myself. *Damn right it's real, and I had better figure out what I'm going to do about it.*"

On September 14, President Bush paid a memorable visit to New York. As he emerged from Air Force One, he asked a tearful Giuliani: "What can I do for you?"

"If you catch this guy, Bin Laden, I would like to be the one to execute him," the mayor replied.

Giuliani later wrote that Bush probably "thought I was just speaking rhetorically, but I was serious."

Two days later, with the New York fire department still reeling from the deaths of 343 men, Giuliani presided over a ceremony promoting 168 members of the department.

"Our hearts are broken, no question about that," he told the firefighters and their families. "But we're going to take out of our hearts' being broken the determination to make this city even more secure."

He added: "Yes, they've taken some of our most precious lives, but they have not taken our spirit. The spirit of democracy is stronger than these cowardly terrorists."

Giuliani had always prided himself on staying rational when those around him become emotional. But after five days of his round-the-clock management of the worst crisis in the city's history, his emotions finally caught up with him.

"For me, that ceremony may have been the single most wrenching moment of the entire crisis," he later wrote. "When it was done, I sat down and the tears just welled up. I did my best to contain them but I couldn't."

One month after of the terrorist attacks, Giuliani gave a tour of Ground Zero to Saudi Prince Alwaleed bin Talal, who handed the mayor a $10 million check for disaster relief. But later that day, the prince released a statement saying America "must address some of the issues that led to such a criminal attack." The statement implied that America had brought the attack on itself.

"I believe the government of the United States of America should re-examine its policies in the Middle East and adopt a more balanced stance toward the Palestinian cause," the prince wrote. "Our Palestinian brethren continue to be slaughtered at the hands of Israelis while the world turns the other cheek."

When Giuliani was told about the prince's statement, he called it "highly irresponsible and very, very dangerous." He added that for the prince to suggest "there's a justification" for the terrorist attacks merely served to invite additional attacks.

"Not only are those statements wrong, they're part of the problem," the mayor said. "One of the reasons I think this happened is because people were engaged in moral equivalency in not understanding the difference between liberal democracies like the United States, like Israel, and terrorist states and those who condone terrorism."

Giuliani refused to cash the check.

"The check has not been deposited," he said. "The Twin Towers Fund has not accepted it."

The mayor privately fretted that some families of victims might think it unwise to give back a gift of $10 million. But his worries proved baseless.

"Many victims' family members told me they were glad," Giuliani recalled in *Leadership*. "A surprising number of them used the same phrase: 'We don't want his blood money.' Not a single person ever came up to me and said I should have kept it."

Such was the leadership that elevated Rudy Giuliani to heroic status in the aftermath of September 11. As the weeks passed, the accolades piled up. Oprah Winfrey dubbed Giuliani "America's Mayor." Queen Elizabeth made him an honorary knight. *Time* hailed him as a "great leader" and named him "person of the year." Appreciative New Yorkers mobbed the mayor every time he set foot on a sidewalk.

A handful of critics noted that before the terrorist attacks, the mayor's popularity had begun to wane. More than one wag sniped that on September 10, Giuliani couldn't have been elected dog catcher.

"On 9/10/01 he was a bum, on 9/11 he was a man, and on 9/12 he was a hero," wrote Peggy Noonan in the *Wall Street Journal*. "Life can change, shift, upend in an instant."

Whatever the case, Rudy Giuliani ended his mayoralty with sky-high approval ratings and political ambitions to match.

EYES ON THE PRIZE

After leaving office at the end of 2001, Giuliani married Judith
Nathan and set about amassing a personal fortune. He founded
Giuliani Partners, a security firm that raked in $100 million in
consulting and lobbying fees during its first five years. He
began giving speeches that earned him upward of $10 million
a year. He further increased his wealth by joining a Texas law
firm, which became known as Bracewell & Giuliani.

A major supporter of President Bush's aggressive prosecution of the war on terror, Giuliani lavished praise on the commander in chief during a speech at the 2004 Republican
National Convention in New York City.

"No matter what happens in this election, President George
W. Bush already has earned a place in history as a great American president," he told the party faithful. "And since September 11, President Bush has remained rock solid. It doesn't
matter to him how he is demonized. It doesn't matter what
the media does to ridicule him or misinterpret him or defeat
him.

"They ridiculed Winston Churchill. They belittled Ronald
Reagan. But like President Bush, they were optimists. Leaders
need to be optimists. Their vision is beyond the present, and it's
set on a future of real peace and security. Some call it stubborn-
ness. I call it principled leadership. President Bush has the
courage of his convictions."

Even during a vivid retelling of his experiences on September 11, Giuliani managed to plug the president.

"Without really thinking, based on just emotion, spontaneous, I grabbed the arm of then–police commissioner Bernard Kerik, and I said to him, 'Bernie, thank God George Bush is our president.' " Giuliani recalled. "I say it again tonight. I say it again tonight: Thank God that George Bush is our president.

"And thank God that Dick Cheney, a man with his experience and his knowledge and his strength and his background, is our vice president," he added.

After Bush won re-election, he was said to be interested in getting Giuliani to serve as secretary of homeland security. But Giuliani demurred, instead recommending his old friend Kerik. A week after Kerik was nominated, however, he withdrew amid a flurry of personal scandals. Giuliani was widely blamed for embarrassing the president.

In 2006, Giuliani passed up chances to run for governor and the U.S. Senate, preferring to keep his eye on the biggest prize of all—the presidency. He threw his hat into the ring in early 2007 and promptly became the Republican front-runner, consistently outpolling rivals Mitt Romney, Fred Thompson, and John McCain. This puzzled many pundits, who expected Giuliani to be hurt by his liberal social positions. After all, the mayor was an outspoken advocate for gun control and had once likened the National Rifle Association to "extremists." He supported gay rights, marched in gay parades, and publicly appeared in drag on numerous occasions for comedic purposes. Furthermore, Giuliani had been endorsed repeatedly by the Liberal Party of New York. The mayor even endorsed liberal Mario Cuomo in the New York gubernatorial election of 1994, a move that Republican candidate George Pataki likened to "a knife in the back."

Meanwhile, Giuliani's relationship with his two children had become strained. His son, Andrew, a student at Duke University, seemed particularly unhappy with his father's marriage to Judith Nathan.

"There's obviously a little problem that exists between me and his wife," Andrew told the *New York Times.* "And we're trying to figure that out. But as of right now it's not working as well as we would like."

Giuliani's daughter, Caroline, a freshman at Harvard, went so far as to announce on her Facebook website that she was supporting Democrat Barack Obama for president over her own father.

On the plus side, Giuliani's third marriage was going well. "You know, I have a relationship that is very fulfilling and that has given me a much better perspective on life," he told me.

Politically, one of Giuliani's biggest challenges was his disagreement with the Republican Party over abortion.

"See, I don't equate abortion with murdering a child, which I guess puts me in conflict with the teaching of the Catholic Church," he told *New York* magazine in 1987. "There is a moral consequence to the elimination of a fetus, but it's not the same thing as murder."

Two years later, during his unsuccessful mayoral campaign, Giuliani reaffirmed his pro-choice credentials.

"If the ultimate choice of the woman—my daughter or any other woman—would be that in this particular circumstance, to have an abortion, I'd support that," he said on Phil Donahue's TV talk show a week after his daughter was born. "I'd give my daughter the money for it."

He would also give other people's money, in the form of tax dollars, to women who wanted abortions.

"There must be public funding for abortions for poor women," he said during speech that same year. "We cannot deny any woman the right to make her own decision about abortion because she lacks resources."

Giuliani reaffirmed this position eight years later, when he filled out a questionnaire from the National Abortion Rights Action League (NARAL). He answered "yes" to the question "Do you support Medicaid funding for abortion without any restrictions?"

But when he started running for president, Giuliani said he opposes federal funding of abortions. He even voiced support for the Hyde amendment, which bans such funding. However, he still supported taxpayer financing at the state level.

"So you support taxpayer money, or public funding, for abortion, in some cases?" CNN's Dana Bash asked Giuliani in 2007.

"If it would deprive someone of a constitutional right, yes," he replied.

In the same interview, Giuliani made a point of repeating his mantra that "abortion's wrong, abortion shouldn't happen." Yet throughout the 1990s, he and his second wife, Donna Hanover, gave money at least half a dozen times to Planned Parenthood, the nation's top provider of abortions. I asked him to explain this seeming contradiction.

"Those were contributions that were made by my wife and by me at the time," Giuliani told me. "I can't remember exactly the reasons for them, but Planned Parenthood, I also always thought, is an organization that made information available about adoption."

There are other inconsistencies in Giuliani's abortion stance. For example, on the 1997 NARAL questionnaire, he also answered "yes" to the questions "Would you oppose a ban on partial-birth abortions?" and "Would you oppose forcing minors to get parental notification before they have an abortion?" But when he began his White House bid, he changed his answer to both of these questions to "no."

Giuliani further muddied the waters during a May 2007 interview on Fox News Channel. Although he was already on record as opposing stem cell research that entailed creating life in order to destroy it, he now refused to say whether frozen embryos constituted life.

"I can't decide when life begins." He shrugged. "All that I can decide is, you know, what are the constitutional issues? What are the legal issues? How do you deal with these things?"

The remark was strikingly similar to one by rival Republican Mitt Romney about when life begins.

"I don't know when the spirit, or the soul, enters the body. And I haven't tried to calculate that," Romney told me. "I'm not looking at a religious definition of life. I'm looking at a civilization's, at a civilized society's definition of when life begins."

Giuliani does not believe that pro-lifers have any moral superiority over pro-choicers.

"I know people who find, as a matter of conscience, abortion to be morally wrong," he told me. "And I know people that are equally as good, equally as responsible, equally as moral, who come to the position that abortion is morally necessary. Not necessarily because they agree with abortion, but because they believe that other people should have a right to run their own lives."

Giuliani said he doesn't take it personally when pro-lifers say they cannot vote for him because of his abortion stance.

"I think maybe growing up a Catholic, maybe being as knowledgeable as I am about theology and moral theology and everything, I don't get angry at all about people who say, 'Gee, you know, this is the one most important issue to me, and on this issue, there's a difference of conscience,' " he told me. "I just wish, not so much that they'd vote for me, but they'd respect my position."

Giuliani hopes to get credit for sticking to his convictions on abortion, even though he knows his stance is opposed by conservatives. By contrast, Romney changed from pro-choice to pro-life, prompting accusations of political expediency.

"Abortion is an issue on which there will be some people who will just vote against me," Giuliani told me. "I respect people's difference of conscience about abortion—tremendously.

"And if that is the most important issue to you and you feel that I'm the wrong candidate, you have the right to vote against me," he added. "Or you can understand how we can have a difference of opinion on it. Then I'm somebody you can vote for."

IMMIGRATION WORRIES

"I don't consider immigration to be the same as abortion, in the sense that I think that immigration is an issue that is not a negative with any Republican voters for me," Giuliani told me.

Actually, there were more than a few Republicans troubled by Giuliani's immigration record. They pointed to the fact that New York City has long been a haven for hundreds of thousands of illegal immigrants. In fact, instead of deporting them, the city government actually protects them.

In 1989, Democratic mayor Ed Koch issued an executive order forbidding city workers from reporting illegal aliens to federal immigration authorities. The sole exception was for aliens suspected of "engaging in criminal activity" (other than having entered the United States illegally, of course). Koch did not want illegals to be so fearful of deportation that they failed to check themselves into hospitals, send their children to school, or report crimes. This policy was aimed at protecting not just the illegals, but all citizens of New York. After all, criminals who preyed on illegals with impunity would also target legal residents. Crime would rise even further if tens of thousands of children of illegals were running the streets instead of attending schools. Finally, failure to seek hospital treatment could lead to a rise in communicable diseases. So Koch decreed that city services "shall be made available to all aliens." He even ordered city workers to "encourage aliens to make use of those services."

Koch's executive order was reissued by his Democrat successor, David Dinkins, and then by Dinkins's successor, the Republican Giuliani.

"I thought—and I still, to this day, believe—that the Koch practical approach was the right thing to save the lives of the people in my city," Giuliani told me in 2007.

Still, it was a hard sell to conservatives, as the mayor acknowledged in a September 1996 speech.

"I know that our executive order offends some people," he allowed. "They ask: Why should we pay to provide services for illegal immigrants? The answer is: It's not only to protect them, but to protect the rest of society, as well."

He added: "There are times when undocumented immigrants must have a substantial degree of protection."

But such protection meant that significant numbers of lawbreakers—namely, the aliens themselves—were going unpunished.

"We're going to have 400,000, 450,000, maybe more, illegal and undocumented, living in the city of New York, and there's absolutely nothing that I can do about it," Giuliani said in 1996. "The city can't deport them. The state can't deport them. This is a responsibility of the federal government."

But the federal government did not deport 99.5 percent of New York's illegals. In fact, the Immigration and Naturalization Service (INS) deported only 700 to 1,500 of the city's 400,000 aliens each year. And Giuliani said he knew the INS was not about to increase deportation "from 700 or 1,500 to 400,000."

"If they could, I would have turned all the people over. It would have helped me. I would have had a smaller population.

I would have had fewer problems," he told me. "But the practical reality was, they were going to make an infinitesimal, statistically insignificant contribution to the problem. I was stuck with it. And, no matter what their promises, they weren't going to do anything about it."

In fact, according to Giuliani, the INS told his predecessor, Dinkins, to stop reporting criminals for deportation. Dinkins complied, even though he had re-issued Koch's executive order, which called for the reporting of aliens suspected of "engaging in criminal activity." When Giuliani took over as mayor, he wanted to resume the reporting of criminals for deportation. He figured that since the INS was deporting fewer than two thousand illegals per year, they might as well be hardened criminals.

"Why don't you throw out the people who are drug dealers, that are coming out of jail? And before they hit the streets, we can turn them over," Giuliani urged the INS, according to his recollection to me. "We couldn't work that out with them. They wouldn't do it for us. They wouldn't do it for us because they had, you know, some professor with a visa, first, and they had two restaurant workers, and three gardeners. Now it may or may not be right for them to be here, but they're not threatening anybody. These drug dealers are threatening people. I couldn't get them to do that, so I had to handle the thing myself. And I handled it."

Giuliani handled it by adopting a laissez-faire attitude toward the vast majority of illegal immigrants.

"The ones that are causing me no trouble, I'm going to leave them alone," he told me. "They're contributing to the lawful part of the city. I've got so many citizens—legal immigrants, and then some illegal immigrants—committing crimes that I've got to pay attention to them."

Similarly, Giuliani concluded that going after school-age illegals would be an empty political gesture.

"I had sixty to seventy thousand children in school who were illegal immigrants," he told me. "So for the purpose of protecting my backside, I would turn over the names to the immigration service so I could sound like a tough guy? I would end up with fifty to sixty thousand kids on the street. And crime would go up in New York, not go down."

So the mayor resigned himself to the federal government's inability or unwillingness to deport illegals. He absolved himself of any blame for the city's continued status as a haven for four hundred thousand illegals.

"That's the federal government's problem," he told me. "If you're not hurting anybody in my city, I don't care."

But Giuliani's "I don't care" appeasement of illegals sometimes morphed into unabashed cheerleading, as if he were rolling out the red carpet for them.

"Some of the hardest-working and most productive people in this city are undocumented aliens," the mayor said at a 1994 press conference. "If you come here and you work hard and you happen to be in an undocumented status, you're one of the people who we want in this city. You're somebody that we want to protect, and we want you to get out from under what is often a life of being like a fugitive, which is really unfair."

In 2007, I asked Giuliani why it was unfair to apply fugitive status to someone who broke the law to enter the United States and was therefore, by definition, a fugitive.

"We were going to treat them as a fugitive if they committed a crime," he replied. "And we weren't going to treat them like a fugitive if they were being calm and responsible and decent.

"And finally, it didn't much matter what I did with them. The turning over of names to the immigration service was a mere formal act. It was absurd to think that they could possibly handle it. It continues to be absurd," he added. "In order to deal with the twelve million illegals that are in this country, you would have to take the entire federal, state, and local criminal justice systems and multiply it by some factor of seven or eight or nine."

Instead of attempting such an impossible task, Giuliani said he would concentrate on securing the U.S.-Mexico border if elected president.

"The reason I have a plan to stop people at the border is because no other plan will work," he told me in August 2007.

That same month, he assured a South Carolina audience: "We can end illegal immigration. I promise you, we can end illegal immigration."

But back in October 1996, Giuliani dismissed the notion of ending illegal immigration as a pipe dream.

"We're never, ever going to be able to totally control immigration to a country that is as large as ours, that has borders that are as diverse as the borders of the United States," he said in a speech to Harvard's Kennedy School of Government.

"If you were to totally control immigration into the United States," he added, "you might very well destroy the economy of the United States, because you'd have to inspect everything and everyone in every way possible.

"I don't know that there's any technological way to totally control it," he concluded. "You're never totally going to control it, so we have to just accept that if we want to be the kind of country that we are."

In 2007, Giuliani's detractors seized on this line, "we have to just accept that," as proof that he considered border control a hopeless cause. They also sought to portray him as a flip-flopper for initially saying the United States could "never, ever" get control of its borders and then, just a decade later, promising to do just that.

Giuliani countered that advances in technology now made it possible to build an "intelligent" fence along the border. But I pointed out that technology was always advancing. Couldn't he have predicted ten years earlier that such advances would eventually make border security possible?

"No, I couldn't possibly have predicted it ten years ago. I mean, it would have been an unrealistic promise to make to people ten years ago. I don't make unrealistic promises," Giuliani told me. "In the 1980s, which was when most of my ideas for immigration emerged, because I was the third-ranking official in the Justice Department, it would have been inconceivable that you could have covered a two-thousand-mile border—just the southern border—inconceivable, technologically.

"At least it was inconceivable to me, and there was nobody

proposing it," he said. "I didn't have all that knowledge at the time about 360-degree cameras, heat-seeking equipment, motion-detection equipment."

He added: "It's much more doable than people realize. Now, could I have realized that in 1994 or '95? Maybe, I don't know. But I don't think so. And I think if I did, it would have been kind of a future-oriented promise, rather than a reality."

Some of Giuliani's Republican rivals no doubt disagree with his confident assertion that the immigration issue "is not a negative with any Republican voters for me." In fact, after failing to gain traction against Giuliani on such issues as abortion, gays, and guns, these rivals came to view immigration as a potential silver bullet. After all, the issue had proved devastating to Republican John McCain. So fellow Republican Mitt Romney, the former governor of Massachusetts, was eager to wield the immigration issue against Giuliani.

"If you look at lists compiled on websites of sanctuary cities, New York is at the top of the list when Mayor Giuliani was mayor," Romney said. "He instructed city workers not to provide information to the federal government that would allow them to enforce the law. New York City was the poster child for sanctuary cities in the country."

Giuliani disagreed.

"My city wasn't a sanctuary city," he told me when I cited Romney's charge. "He'd be the wrong person to say that, 'cause he had four or five."

By asserting that cities in Massachusetts were soft on immigration during Romney's term as governor, Giuliani hopes to blunt a potentially damaging attack from perhaps his most formidable Republican rival. And in case this counterattack falls short, Giuliani can always pivot to his tough-on-crime credentials.

"My objective was to make New York City safe," he told me. "Illegal immigration and the problem of illegal immigrants was just one of many problems that were part of that whole. So the real question is, did I deal with it intelligently, and did it result in the city becoming much safer? Or did I deal with it stupidly and the city became much more dangerous?"

He believes the answer to that question will calm any fears that voters might harbor about his immigration stance.

"I end up being the strongest candidate on immigration, for the reason that I ran a city and made it real safe," he concluded. "And I don't see any opponent that I have who has ever done nearly as much about bringing down illegality as I have."

"WHY DO YOU SEEM SO HAPPY?"

Giuliani makes little effort to hide his disdain for the leading Democratic presidential candidates.

"Honestly, there is not much difference between Hillary Clinton, Barack Obama, and John Edwards," he told me. "They're all for high taxes, they're all for bigger government, they're all for socialized medicine."

He added that all the Democrats want to play "defense against Islamic terrorism."

"If the country feels that it's in trouble, there's a certain advantage to somebody who has certain achievements," he told me. "America is very concerned about safety and security. I've had the most responsibility, of any of the presidential candidates, for safety and security. I've had that weight on my shoulders. And I've shown I know what to do about it."

The take-no-prisoners former prosecutor has also shown that he has mellowed a bit with age. He attributes this to a confluence of life-changing events.

"People ask me, 'Why do you seem so happy? You seem different than you used to be when you were the mayor, at least in the early days,'" Giuliani told me.

"I think it's cancer, September 11, and Judith," he said. Those three things, according to Giuliani, were more important than running for president. "I think maybe if those things hadn't happened to me, it'd be *too* important," he said of his candidacy.

He added: "I'm just a much more comfortable person. Much more able to see where it all fits. You know, it's not all about politics."

Such serenity was reminiscent of George W. Bush, who made clear in 2000 that if he didn't win the presidency, his life would still go on and he would still be happy. By contrast, his opponent, Al Gore, was portrayed as having spent his life preparing for the presidency.

"I'm very comfortable with the fact that whatever happens in this election, it's the will of God and the will of the people," Giuliani told me. "If I'm going to be president of the United States, it's the will of God and the will of the American people. And if I'm not, all I want to do is my very best job campaigning for it, and elevate things, and try to get ideas out there and thoughts out there."

On the other hand, there's no denying that Rudy Giuliani relishes the prospect of winning the highest office in the land.

"This is what I'm good at," he told me in conclusion. "This is what I know how to do. I know how to lead, I know how to manage, I know how to inspire and I know how to run for office.

"I'm not perfect in any of those things. I've got pluses and minuses. But in the context of all the people available, my pluses and minuses are pretty good."

WHERE RUDY GIULIANI STANDS
ON THE ISSUES

ABORTION
Once opposed a ban on partial-birth abortion but now supports it. Supports taxpayer funding of abortion for poor women.

CLIMATE CHANGE
"I do believe there's global warming," he says, adding that the debate "is almost unnecessary . . . because we should be dealing with pollution anyway."

GAY MARRIAGE
Opposes a constitutional ban. "I'm pro–gay rights."

HEALTH CARE

Opposes government-mandated universal health care. "We can reduce costs and improve the quality of care by increasing competition."

IMMIGRATION

Once said it was impossible to stop illegal immigration, but now says technology has made it possible to seal the border with Mexico.

IRAQ

Strongly supports President Bush's policy.

TAXES

As mayor, reduced taxes in New York by several billion dollars.

4

BARACK OBAMA

B arack Obama, by his own admission, is the ultimate political Rorschach test.

"I am new enough on the national political scene that I serve
as a blank screen on which people of vastly different political
stripes project their own views," he observes. "As such, I am
bound to disappoint some, if not all, of them."

Such candid self-awareness abounds in Obama's two best-
selling memoirs, *Dreams from My Father* and *The Audacity of
Hope.* If nothing else, the books have established the Illinois
Democrat as certainly the best writer in the 2008 presidential
campaign. Indeed, Obama might have been more circumspect
in writing his first book, *Dreams,* if he had known at the time
that he would one day run for president. The volume is filled

with the racial angst of a young man haunted by his black father's abandonment of his white mother.

Americans tend to elect sunny, optimistic presidents who seem capable of uniting the nation. So it remains unclear whether Obama will be hurt by his brooding prose about "white people's scorn" and "all the traps that seem laid in a black man's soul." Perhaps voters will find something refreshing about a candidate who describes himself as "an American with the blood of Africa coursing through my veins." After all, as Obama points out, "Shortly after 2050, experts project, America will no longer be a majority white country."

Obama is equally frank about "my fierce ambitions" for the presidency. But as John Kerry and Al Gore discovered in the last two presidential contests, ambitions are not votes.

UNCONVENTIONAL BACKGROUND

In what has to be one of the biggest coincidences of the 2008 presidential campaign, Barack Obama, like Mitt Romney, is the great-grandson of a polygamist who had five wives.

Obama's busy forefather, also named Obama, was born in 1895, orphaned as a young boy, and grew up to become a farmer near Lake Victoria. His first wife died young, so Obama married her sister, Nyaoke, and, eventually, three other women, all of whom had children.

Nyaoke's fifth son was named Hussein Onyango Obama, who grew up to become a domestic servant for wealthy whites. This fact would one day disappoint his grandson, the presidential candidate, who had imagined his grandfather to be "an in-

dependent man, a man of his people, opposed to white rule."
When Barack learned the truth during a 1988 visit to Kenya, it
caused "ugly words to flash across my mind. Uncle Tom. Col-
laborator. House nigger."

During that same visit, Barack also learned that his grand-
father, who died in 1979, had been fiercely devoted to Islam.
His devotion was described by one of his surviving wives,
Sarah, and recorded by Barack in *Dreams.*

"What your grandfather respected was strength. Discipline," Barack quoted the widow as telling him. "This is also
why he rejected the Christian religion, I think. For a brief time,
he converted, and even changed his name to Johnson. But he
could not understand such ideas as mercy toward your enemies,
or that this man Jesus could wash away a man's sins. To your
grandfather, this was foolish sentiment, something to comfort
women. And so he converted to Islam—he thought its practices conformed more closely to his beliefs."

Onyango married at least four women, including Sarah,
age sixteen, and Akumu, who gave birth to a son, Barack Hussein Obama Sr. Abandoned by his mother at age nine, the boy
was raised by Sarah, who described her stepson as "wild and
stubborn."

"My father grew up herding his father's goats and attending
the local school, set up by the British colonial administration,
where he had shown great promise," Obama Jr. wrote in
Dreams.

By the time he was twenty-three, Obama Sr. had a wife,
Kezia, and son, Roy. When Kezia was pregnant with their second child, Obama Sr. abandoned the family in 1959 to move to

the United States and accept a scholarship at the University of Hawaii. The following year, in a Russian-language course, he met an eighteen-year-old white woman with the unusual name of Stanley Ann Dunham (her father, also named Stanley, had desperately wanted a boy). Dunham, who went by the name of Ann, was a liberal feminist from Kansas. She was also an atheist.

"Her memories of the Christians who populated her youth were not fond ones," her son later wrote. "For my mother, organized religion too often dressed up closed-mindedness in the garb of piety, cruelty and oppression in the cloak of righteousness."

Unfazed by the fact that Obama Sr. already had a wife and children back in Africa, Dunham agreed to marry him. When news of the forthcoming nuptials reached Africa, the father of the groom fired off a letter to the father of the bride, "saying he didn't want his son marrying white," according to Obama Jr.'s account in *Dreams*. Dunham's parents, while taken aback, did not stop their daughter from marrying black.

"Like most white people at the time, they had never really given black people much thought," Obama Jr. wrote in *Dreams*. "Would you let your daughter marry one? The fact that my grandparents had answered yes to this question, no matter how grudgingly, remains an enduring puzzle to me."

So, within a year of meeting Obama Sr., Dunham was married and pregnant.

"He was black as pitch, my mother white as milk," Obama Jr. wrote in *Dreams*. "In many parts of the South, my father could have been strung up from a tree for merely looking at my mother the wrong way; in the most sophisticated of northern cities, the hostile stares, the whispers, might have driven a woman in my mother's predicament into a back-alley abortion."

But she did not abort Barack Hussein Obama Jr., who was born in Honolulu on August 4, 1961, into a decidedly nonreligious household.

"Although my father had been raised a Muslim, by the time he met my mother he was a confirmed atheist," wrote Obama, who nonetheless cited Islam when explaining his own first name. "It means 'Blessed.' In Arabic. My grandfather was a Muslim."

Young Barack's Americanized moniker became Barry, which was often shortened by family members to Bar. His parents planned to move the family to Kenya after Obama Sr. finished his studies. But when Barry reached the tender age of two, his father left the family to accept another scholarship, this one at Harvard. He did not return to Hawaii, where his wife filed for divorce. Obama Sr. eventally married a white woman named Ruth and lived with her in Kenya, where he reclaimed his two children from his first wife, telling them that Ruth was now their mother. Obama Sr. went to work for Shell Oil Company and prospered.

Obama Jr. later traced "the sense of abandonment I'd felt as a boy" to the fact that his father deserted him before "my own memories begin." He harbored a "fantasy of the Old Man's having taken my mother and me back with him to Kenya." He looked back on "a past that left me feeling exposed, even slightly ashamed," noting: "I was too young to realize that I was supposed to have a live-in father, just as I was too young to know that I needed a race."

Obama would long be troubled by his mixed-race identity and the fact his father had abandoned him. In fact, these two festering psychological wounds would come to define his very existence. He became acutely conscious of his own angst, even imagining that others could see the "tragedy" of "my troubled heart." He brooded over "the mixed blood, the divided soul, the ghostly image of the tragic mulatto trapped between two worlds."

When Obama was six, his mother married another foreign student at the University of Hawaii, Lolo Soetoro of Indonesia, and the family moved to Jakarta. As a stranger in a strange land, young Barack found himself "puzzling out the meaning of the muezzin's call to evening prayer" and other mysteries. He became almost completely dependent on his new stepfather.

"It was to Lolo that I turned to for guidance and instruction," he recalled in *Dreams*.

Still, it took Obama "less than six months to learn Indonesia's language, its customs and its legends," he recalled. It was such a "rapid acculturation," Obama wrote, that he was soon participating in "the goose-stepping demonstrations my Indonesian Boy Scout troop performed in front of the president."

Even his diet changed.

"I was introduced to dog meat (tough), snake meat (tougher), and roasted grasshopper (crunchy)," Obama wrote in *Dreams*. "Like many Indonesians, Lolo followed a brand of Islam that could make room for the remnants of more ancient animist and Hindu faiths. He explained that a man took on the powers of whatever he ate: One day soon, he promised, he would bring home a piece of tiger meat for us to share."

Although his mother was an atheist, young Obama was not shielded from religion. "In our household, the Bible, the Koran, and the Bhagavad Gita sat on the shelf," he later recalled. He spent his first two years in Indonesia attending a Catholic school, then "spent two years at a Muslim school," he wrote.

The latter taught the Koran, Islam's holy book, along with subjects such as math and science. "The teacher wrote to tell my mother that I made faces during Koranic studies," Obama recalled in *Dreams*.

"RACIAL OBSESSIONS"

As he grew older, Obama became more self-conscious about his race.

"I noticed that there was nobody like me in the Sears, Roebuck Christmas catalogue," he wrote in *Dreams*. "And that Santa was a white man."

Obama's mother eventually gave birth to a girl, Maya, in Indonesia, although Ann's marriage to Lolo later failed and she returned to Honolulu with her two children. Barack began fifth grade at Punahou, which he described as "a prestigious prep school, an incubator for island elites." At Christmastime, Obama's missing father, Barack Obama Sr., visited the family for the first and only time. He had sired four more sons in Kenya, two by his first wife, Kezia, and two by his third, Ruth. But Ruth had just left Obama Sr., who now suggested a reunion with Ann. This suggestion was rejected because, for starters, Ann had not yet divorced Lolo. So after a somewhat tense, month-long visit, Obama Sr. departed, never to be seen by his Hawaiian family again.

Three years later, Ann returned to Indonesia, taking Maya with her. Young Barack chose to remain in Hawaii with his maternal grandparents, noting: "During my teenage years I would return to Indonesia three or four times on short visits."

By this time, Barack's self-described "racial obsessions" were in full bloom. He complained of a "constant, crippling fear that I didn't belong somehow, that unless I dodged and hid and pretended to be something I wasn't I would forever remain an outsider, with the rest of the world, black and white, always standing in judgment."

Obama said he punched out "the first boy, in seventh grade, who called me a coon." Writing in *Dreams,* he vividly recalled the bigot's "tears of surprise—'Why'dya do that?'—when I gave him a bloody nose."

He added: "I ceased to advertise my mother's race at the age of twelve or thirteen, when I began to suspect that by doing so I was ingratiating myself to whites."

And yet even through high school, he continued to vacillate between the twin strands of his racial identity.

"I learned to slip back and forth between my black and white worlds," he wrote in *Dreams.* "One of those tricks I had learned: People were satisfied so long as you were courteous and smiled and made no sudden moves. They were more than satisfied; they were relieved—such a pleasant surprise to find a well-mannered young black man who didn't seem angry all the time."

Despite the fact that Obama spent various portions of his youth living with his white maternal grandfather and Indonesian stepfather, he vowed that he would "never emulate white men and brown men whose fates didn't speak to my own. It was into my father's image, the black man, son of Africa, that I'd packed all the attributes I sought in myself, the attributes of Martin and Malcolm, DuBois and Mandela."

Obama was particularly drawn to the writings of Malcolm X, an influential American Muslim who served as the spokesman for the militant Nation of Islam.

"Malcolm X's autobiography seemed to offer something different," Obama wrote. "His repeated acts of self-creation spoke to me; the blunt poetry of his words, his unadorned insistence on respect, promised a new and uncompromising order, martial in its discipline, forged through sheer force of will."

He added: "If Malcolm's discovery toward the end of his life, that some whites might live beside him as brothers in Islam, seemed to offer some hope of eventual reconciliation, that hope appeared in a distant future, in a far-off land."

Obama described himself as "disaffected" during his last two years of high school. Like many, he sought solace in drugs.

"Pot has helped, and booze; maybe a little blow when you could afford it," he wrote in *Dreams*. "Not smack, though."

Obama was a casual user of cocaine, and wrote that he even came close to trying heroin. In fact, he went so far as to enter the freezer of a delicatessen with "my potential initiator," a junkie who "pulled out the needle and tubing" for Obama.

"Right then an image popped into my head of an air bubble, shiny and round like a pearl, rolling quietly through a vein and stopping my heart," recalled Obama, who got cold feet and declined the heroin.

Instead, Obama turned to basketball and even made the high-school varsity squad.

"It was there that I would make my closest white friends, on turf where blackness couldn't be a disadvantage," he recalled. "I was living out a caricature of black male adolescence, itself a caricature of swaggering American manhood."

And yet even the basketball court proved no refuge from racism. He once heard an assistant basketball coach refer to a group of black men as "niggers."

"I told him—with a fury that surprised even me—to shut up," Obama wrote.

"There are black people, and there are niggers," the coach explained, according to Obama. "Those guys were niggers."

Obama answered with contempt.

" 'There are white folks and then there are ignorant motherf—ers like you,' I had finally told the coach before walking off the court," he wrote.

The exchange appeared to reinforce Obama's distrust of whites.

"That's just how white folks will do you," he wrote. "It wasn't merely the cruelty involved; I was learning that black people could be mean and then some. It was a particular brand of arrogance, an obtuseness in otherwise sane people that brought forth our bitter laughter. It was as if whites didn't know they were being cruel in the first place. Or at least thought you deserving of their scorn."

Obama wrote that he and a black friend in high school would sometimes speak disparagingly "about white folks this or white folks that, and I would suddenly remember my mother's smile, and the words that I spoke would seem awkward and false." Obama recalls telling his friend to "give the bad-assed nigger pose a rest. Save it for when we really needed it." He concluded that "certain whites could be excluded from the general category of our distrust."

Donna Brazile, who managed former vice president Al Gore's presidential campaign in 2000, said Obama's feelings of distrust toward most whites and doubts about himself are fairly typical for black Americans.

"He was a young man trying to discover, trying to accept, trying to come to grips with his background," she told me. "In the process, he had to really make some statements that are hurtful, maybe. But I think they're more insightful than anything."

Obama's candid racial revelations abound in *Dreams,* which was first published in 1995, when he was thirty-four and not yet in politics. By the time he ran for the U.S. Senate in 2004, he observed of that first memoir: "Certain passages have proven to be inconvenient politically."

Thus, in his second memoir, *The Audacity of Hope,* which was published in 2005, Obama took a more conciliatory, even upbeat tone when discussing race.

"I have witnessed a profound shift in race relations in

my lifetime," he wrote. "I insist that things have gotten better."

This appears to contradict certain passages in his first memoir, including a description of the white race as "that ghostly figure that haunted black dreams."

"That hate hadn't gone away," he wrote, blaming "white people—some cruel, some ignorant, sometimes a single face, sometimes just a faceless image of a system claiming power over our lives."

There are other stark differences in the racial tones of Obama's first and second memoirs. For instance, in the second memoir, when discussing his multiracial family, Obama wrote: "I've never had the option of restricting my loyalties on the basis of race, or measuring my worth on the basis of tribe."

But in his first memoir, Obama took the opposite stance, as evidenced in his description of black student life at Occidental College in Los Angeles.

"There were enough of us on campus to constitute a tribe, and when it came to hanging out many of us chose to function like a tribe, staying close together, traveling in packs," he wrote. "It remained necessary to prove which side you were on, to show your loyalty to the black masses, to strike out and name names."

He added: "To avoid being mistaken for a sellout, I chose my friends carefully. The more politically active black students. The foreign students. The Chicanos. The Marxist professors and structural feminists."

Obama said he and other blacks were careful not to second-guess their own racial identity in front of whites.

"To admit our doubt and confusion to whites, to open up our psyches to general examination by those who had caused so much of the damage in the first place, seemed ludicrous, itself an expression of self-hatred," he wrote.

While at Occidental, Obama was assigned to read Joseph Conrad's *Heart of Darkness*.

"It is a racist book. The way Conrad sees it, Africa's the cesspool of the world, black folks are savages, and any contact with them breeds infection," Obama concluded. "I read the book to help me understand just what it is that makes white people so afraid. Their demons. The way ideas get twisted around. It helps me understand how people learn to hate."

After his sophomore year, Obama transferred to Columbia University. He lived on Manhattan's Upper East Side, venturing to the East Village for "the socialist conferences I sometimes attended at Cooper Union," he recalled, adding: "Much of what I absorbed from the sixties was filtered through my mother, who to the end of her life would proudly proclaim herself an unreconstructed liberal."

Back at his apartment, he would sit on his fire escape and "watch white people from the better neighborhoods nearby walk their dogs down our block to let the animals shit on our curbs," Obama wrote. " 'Scoop the poop, you bastards!' my roommate would shout with impressive rage, and we'd laugh at the faces of both master and beast, grim and unapologetic as they hunkered down to do the deed. I enjoyed such moments."

Later, looking back on his years in New York City, he recalled: "I had grown accustomed, everywhere, to suspicions between the races."

FULFILLING WORK

Obama graduated from Columbia in 1983 with a political science degree and joined what he called a "consulting house to multinational corporations." He became a writer and financial analyst for Business International Corporation, an employer he immediately distrusted.

"Like a spy behind enemy lines, I arrived every day at my mid-Manhattan office and sat at my computer terminal, checking the Reuters machine that blinked bright emerald messages from across the globe," he recalled. "I had my own office, my own secretary, money in the bank. Sometimes, coming out of an interview with Japanese financiers or German bond traders, I would catch my reflection in the elevator doors—see myself in a suit and tie, a briefcase in my hand—and for a split second I would imagine myself as a captain of industry, barking out orders, closing the deal, before I remembered who it was that I had told myself I wanted to be and felt pangs of guilt for my lack of resolve."

He added: "As far as I could tell I was the only black man in the company, a source of shame for me."

Obama quit after a year to find more satisfying work.

"I spent three months working for a Ralph Nader offshoot up in Harlem, trying to convince the minority students at City College about the importance of recycling," he wrote in *Dreams*. "In search of some inspiration, I went to hear Kwame Toure, formerly Stokely Carmichael of SNCC and Black Panther fame, speak at Columbia. At the entrance to the auditorium,

two women, one black, one Asian, were selling Marxist literature."

Although Obama had disapproved of what he called fellow
"half-breeds" who gravitated toward whites instead of blacks
in college, he now found himself gravitating the same way.

"There was a woman in New York that I loved. She was
white," he wrote in *Dreams*. "We saw each other for almost a
year. On the weekends, mostly. Sometimes in her apartment,
sometimes in mine. You know how you can fall into your own
private world? Just two people, hidden and warm. Your own
language. Your own customs."

But there was no getting around their racial differences,
which ultimately doomed the relationship.

"I pushed her away," Obama recalled. "I realized that our
two worlds, my friend's and mine, were as distant from each
other as Kenya is from Germany. And I knew that if we stayed
together, I'd eventually live in hers. After all, I'd been doing it
most of my life. Between the two of us, I was the one who knew
how to live as an outsider."

He added: "The emotion between the races could never be
pure; even love was tarnished by the desire to find in the other
some element that was missing in ourselves. Whether we
sought out our demons or salvation, the other race would always remain just that: menacing, alien, and apart."

In June 1985, Obama was interviewed in New York by
Marty Kaufman, a community organizer from Chicago.

"He was trying to pull urban blacks and suburban whites
together around a plan to save manufacturing jobs in metro-

politan Chicago. He needed somebody to work with him, he said. Somebody black," Obama recalled. "There was something about him that made me wary. A little too sure of himself, maybe. And white."

Nonetheless, Obama took the job and moved to Chicago's South Side, where his "racial obsessions" seemed only to intensify. He even asked himself whether "hatred of whites" served any purpose.

"Ever since the first time I'd picked up Malcolm X's autobiography, I had tried to untangle the twin strands of black nationalism, arguing that nationalism's affirmative message—of solidarity and self-reliance, discipline and communal responsibility—need not depend on hatred of whites any more than it depended on white munificence."

But he added: "In talking to self-professed nationalists . . . I came to see how the blanket indictment of everything white served a central function in their message of uplift."

Of course, as the son of a white woman, Obama was ambivalent about any ideology premised on "the blanket indictment of everything white." And yet he couldn't help but see the merits of black nationalism.

"Desperate times called for desperate measures, and for many blacks, times were chronically desperate. If nationalism could create a strong and effective insularity, deliver on its promise of self-respect, then the hurt it might cause well-meaning whites, or the inner turmoil it caused people like me, would be of little consequence," he wrote. "It was this unyielding reality—that white were not simply phantoms to be expunged from our dreams but were an active and varied fact of our everyday lives—that finally explained how nationalism could thrive as an emotion and flounder as a program."

He added: "Among the handful of groups to hoist the nationalist banner, only the Nation of Islam had any significant following: Minister Farrakhan's sharply cadenced sermons generally drew a packed house, and still more listened to his radio broadcasts."

In *Dreams,* Obama cited "the much-admired success of the Nation of Islam in turning around the lives of drug addicts and criminals. But if it was especially well suited to those at the bottom rungs of American life, it also spoke to all the continuing doubts of the lawyer who had run hard for the gold ring yet still experienced the awkward silence when walking into the clubhouse."

By this point in his life, Obama had a keen understanding of the role that race could play in politics.

"Black politicians," he wrote, "discovered what white politicians had known for a very long time: that race-baiting could make up for a host of limitations."

He added: "Black rage always found a ready market."

Obama made clear that such rage was driven, in part, by Republican policies.

"Ronald Reagan was doing quite well with his brand of verbal legerdemain, and white America seemed ever willing to spend vast sums of money on suburban parcels and private security forces to deny the indissoluble link between black and white," he lamented. "We sank into further despair."

FINDING RELIGION, ROOTS

Meanwhile, Obama's job required him to work with numerous Chicago churches, where parishioners noticed that he did not share their religious faith. He was repeatedly asked to join Christian congregations, but begged off.

"I remained a reluctant skeptic, doubtful of my own motives, wary of expedient conversion, having too many quarrels with God to accept a salvation too easily won," he wrote. "I had no community or shared traditions in which to ground my most deeply held beliefs."

But he did have an aversion to what he called "the religious absolutism of the Christian right." He wrote that such believers insist "not only that Christianity is America's dominant faith, but that a particular, fundamentalist brand of that faith should drive public policy, overriding any alternative source of understanding, whether the writings of liberal theologians, the findings of the National Academy of Sciences, or the words of Thomas Jefferson."

Although the overwhelming majority of Americans describe themselves as Christians, Obama did not believe that any one religion should define the United States.

"We are no longer just a Christian nation," he argued in *Audacity*. "We are also a Jewish nation, a Muslim nation, a Buddhist nation, a Hindu nation, and a nation of nonbelievers."

Although Obama's father, stepfather, brother, and grandfather were Muslims, and Obama himself had been fascinated by the Nation of Islam, he decided to become a Christian. He attributed this to "the particular attributes of the historically black church, attributes that helped me shed some of my skepticism and embrace the Christian faith."

But Obama, a staunch liberal, did not join the sort of socially conservative church that is frequently found in the black community. Instead, he joined Trinity United Church of Christ on Chicago's South Side, which was led by a radical leftist, the Reverend Jeremiah A. Wright Jr. Routinely denouncing the United States as a "racist" and "imperialistic" nation dominated by "white arrogance," Wright advocated a redistribution of wealth that went beyond socialism. The congregation was required to embrace "economic parity" and disavow "the pursuit of 'middleclassness.' " Above all, the militant, Afrocentric church insisted on what it calls "a non-negotiable commitment to Africa."

Best of all, Obama wrote, Trinity was a church where "religious commitment did not require me to suspend critical thinking, disengage from the battle for economic and social justice, or otherwise retreat from the world I knew and loved." So he joined and became a Christian.

"I was finally able to walk down the aisle of Trinity United Church of Christ one day and be baptized," he recalled. "It came about as a choice and not an epiphany; the questions I had did not magically disappear. But kneeling beneath that cross on the South Side of Chicago, I felt God's spirit beckoning me. I submitted myself to His will, and dedicated myself to discovering His truth."

In 1988, after three years of community organizing in Chicago, Obama made his first visit to Kenya, where his father had died in a car accident half a dozen years earlier. In typical fashion, he viewed the trip with an abundance of racial trepidation. He brooded about "my own uneasy status: a Westerner not entirely at home in the West, an African on his way to a land full of strangers."

But when he arrived, Obama found it refreshing to be in the racial majority.

"You could experience the freedom that comes from not being watched, the freedom of believing that your hair grows as it's supposed to grow and that your rump sways the way a rump is supposed to sway," he marveled. "Here the world was black, and so you were just you; you could discover all those things that were unique to your life without living a lie or committing betrayal."

Obama shared moonshine while reminiscing with long-lost relatives. He wrote that he found it "intoxicating" to gaze at "the entrance to an open-air mosque, where we watched a group of bank officers carefully remove their wing-tipped shoes and bathe their feet before joining farmers and ditchdiggers in afternoon prayer."

Still, he wasn't fond of white tourists, whom he considered "an encroachment."

"They were everywhere—Germans, Japanese, British, American," he groused. "Some came because Kenya, without shame, offered to re-create an age when the lives of whites in foreign lands rested comfortably on the backs of the darker races."

Upon reaching his father's gravesite, Obama was told by his brother, Roy, that "the government wanted a Christian burial. The family wanted a Muslim burial."

"A CERTAIN MEGOLOMANIA"

Returning to America, Obama decided not to resume his community organizing in Chicago.

"I went to Harvard Law School, spending most of three years in poorly lit libraries, poring through cases and statutes," he wrote in *Dreams*.

After his first year, he was hired as a "summer associate" at a big corporate law firm in Chicago, Sidley & Austin. He was assigned a mentor, Michelle Robinson, a twenty-four-year-old practicing attorney who had already graduated from Harvard Law. Obama was smitten, but Robinson initially refused to date him because she was his adviser. Eventually, she relented.

Obama later was elected the first black president of the *Harvard Law Review*. This brought him "some modest publicity," he recalled, which in turn led to a publishing deal to write his first memoir, *Dreams from My Father*.

After graduating from Harvard, Obama spent most of 1992 running a voter registration drive in Chicago. In October, he married Michelle at Trinity United in Chicago in a ceremony attended by some of Obama's African siblings.

"The person who made me proudest of all," Obama wrote, "was Roy. Actually, now we call him Abongo, his Luo name, for two years ago he decided to reassert his African heritage. He converted to Islam, and has sworn off pork and tobacco and alcohol."

Obama added: "His conversion has given him solid ground to stand on, a pride in his place in the world." However, there was also a new "tension. He's prone to make lengthy pronouncements on the need for the black man to liberate himself from the poisoning influences of European culture."

In 1993, Obama joined a Chicago law firm and became a lecturer at the University of Chicago Law School. He continued working on his first book, *Dreams,* which was published in 1995. "Sales were underwhelming," he noted, unaware of the bestseller status that would accompany his entry into national politics years later.

But first he entered state politics. In 1996, Obama was elected to the Illinois state Senate, winning re-election two years later. Setting his sights on the U.S. Congress, he made the mistake of challenging the wildly popular congressman Bobby Rush of Chicago in the Democratic primary of 2000.

"Less than halfway into the campaign, I knew in my bones that I was going to lose," Obama wrote in *Audacity.* "I arrived at my victory party to discover that the race had already been called and that I had lost by thirty-one points."

Years later, Obama still burned with the thought of his only loss in politics, which he called a "drubbing." It reminded him that politicians are driven by a combination of ambition and fear.

"Not just fear of losing—although that is bad enough—but fear of total, complete humiliation," he wrote. "In politics, there may be second acts, but there is no second place."

On October 2, 2002, ten days before the U.S. Senate planned to vote on an Iraq War resolution, Obama warned that such a conflict would be a catastrophic mistake.

"Even a successful war against Iraq will require a U.S. occupation of undetermined length, at undetermined cost, with undetermined consequences," he said at an antiwar rally in Chicago. "I know that an invasion of Iraq without a clear rationale and without strong international support will only fan the flames of the Middle East, and encourage the worst, rather than best, impulses of the Arab world, and strengthen the recruitment arm of al Qaeda. I am not opposed to all wars. I'm opposed to dumb wars."

This was not a popular position to take just one year after the terrorist attacks of September 11. Democratic senators Hillary Rodham Clinton and John Edwards ended up voting for the war resolution, although both would profoundly regret their votes as the 2008 presidential election approached. By contrast, Obama's early opposition to the war would gradually come to be viewed as prescient by liberal voters.

In 2004, while still a state senator in Illinois, Obama was asked to deliver a keynote address at the Democratic National Convention in Boston. The speech was devoid of the angst that had dominated Obama's early writings. He now chose to paper over the nation's racial differences.

"There is not a black America and white America and Latino America and Asian America; there is the United States of America," he said. "We are one people, all of us pledging allegiance to the stars and stripes, all of us defending the United States of America."

It was Obama's first major national exposure and he wowed the party faithful, many of whom gushed that a political star had been born. The fawning press coverage gave Obama a major boost in his latest political campaign, a bid for the U.S. Senate.

"It requires a certain megalomania, a belief that of all the gifted people in your state, you are somehow uniquely qualified to speak on their behalf," he observed.

It also requires "breathtaking" amounts of money, he quickly learned. "Without money, and the television ads that consume all the money, you are pretty much guaranteed to lose," he added.

"As a consequence of my fundraising, I became more like like the wealthy donors I met," he acknowledged. "I can't assume the money chase didn't alter me in some ways. Certainly it eliminated any sense of shame I once had in asking strangers for large sums of money. By the end of the campaign, the banter and small talk that had once accompanied my solicitation calls were eliminated. I cut to the chase and tried not to take no for an answer."

At least Obama didn't have to worry about the media.

"For a three-year span, from the time that I announced my candidacy for the Senate to the end of my first year as a senator, I was the beneficiary of unusually—and at times undeservedly—positive press coverage. No doubt some of this had to do with my status as an underdog in my Senate primary, as well as my novelty as a black candidate with an exotic background. Maybe it also has something to do with my style of communicating, which can be rambling, hesitant, and overly verbose (both my staff and Michelle often remind me of this), but which perhaps finds sympathy in the literary class."

He added: "I've watched the press cast me in a light that can be hard to live up to."

In addition to getting a free ride from the media, Obama

was blessed with political opponents who self-destructed. He won the Democratic primary after watching his top rival "flame out" because of an "unflattering divorce file," Obama conceded. Then his Republican opponent "was felled by a divorce scandal of his own," he added.

"There was no point in denying my almost spooky good fortune," he acknowledged. "To political insiders, my victory proved nothing."

As a senator, Obama frequently made a point of finding something charitable to say about his opponents' arguments, yet almost always ended up voting liberal.

"The arguments of liberals are more often grounded in reason and fact," he wrote in *Audacity*.

Obama has a 95 percent liberal rating from Americans for Democratic Reform, a liberal advocacy group that ranks all members of Congress. Yet he is often portrayed as a centrist.

"His record is liberal and his rhetoric is moderate," explained Larry Sabato, director of the University of Virginia's center for politics.

For example, Obama went out of his way to voice approval of at least some aspects of Ronald Reagan's presidency.

"At times, in arguments with some of my friends on the left, I would find myself in the curious position of defending aspects of Reagan's worldview," he wrote in *Audacity*. "When the Berlin Wall came tumbling down, I had to give the old man his due, even if I never gave him my vote."

But in summing up Reagan, Obama concluded that the former president's "clarity about communism seemed matched by his blindness regarding other sources of misery in the world."

By pointing out the merits of both sides of an argument, Obama could at times sound statesmanlike, even if he almost never actually sided with conservatives. This dichotomy could also be seen in Obama's analysis of President Bush's foreign policy.

"I agree with George W. Bush when in his second inaugural address he proclaimed a universal desire to be free," Obama wrote. "But there are few examples in history in which the freedom men and women crave is delivered through outside intervention."

In January 2007, with just two years of experience in the Senate, Obama threw his hat into the presidential ring. Almost immediately, he eclipsed John Edwards, who had been toiling on his own White House bid for two years, as the leading Democratic alternative to front-runner Hillary Rodham Clinton. Even Clinton was forced to react to Obama's entry into the race by announcing her own candidacy just days later. Thus began a historic struggle between the first woman and the first black to have realistic shots at the presidency.

Mindful of his relative inexperience, Obama cast himself as the candidate of change. But he made a series of early gaffes on foreign policy that allowed Clinton to emphasize the importance of her long years of experience.

Meanwhile, Obama had found that the press was not as fawning as it had been during his Senate campaign. He lamented "the growth of an unabashedly partisan press: talk radio, Fox News, newspaper editorialists, the cable talk-show circuit, and most recently the bloggers, all of them trading insults, accusations, gossip, and innuendo twenty-four hours a day, seven days a week."

"The constant vitriol can wear on the spirit," he wrote in *Audacity*. "Oddly enough, the cruder broadsides you don't worry about too much; if Rush Limbaugh's listeners enjoy hearing him call me 'Osama Obama,' my attitude is, let them have their fun."

Obama's wife, Michelle, now the mother of two daughters, objected to pundits who often asked of her husband: Is he black enough? Yet the question was also asked and answered by Obama supporters, including civil rights leader Roger Wilkins, who introduced Obama at a speech by telling the liberal audience: "This man is black enough, I guarantee you."

Obama didn't bother pointing out that he had once described his father as "black," but himself as "brown." He didn't tell the audience that a Manhattan publisher had once reminded him that he didn't "come from an underprivileged background."

Instead, Obama was content to be as black as people wanted him to be, knowing that he could never satisfy everyone's racial expectations.

"I can't even hold up my experience as being somehow representative of the black American experience," he conceded before adding: "I can embrace my black brothers and sisters, whether in this country or in Africa, and affirm a common destiny without pretending to speak to, or for, all our various struggles."

Ultimately, however, Barack Obama will have to demonstrate that he can also embrace whites and other races if he wants to be the next president.

WHERE BARACK OBAMA STANDS
ON THE ISSUES

ABORTION

Pro-choice. As a state senator in Illinois, he voted against a ban on partial birth abortion.

CLIMATE CHANGE

Supports mandatory 80 percent cuts in emissions by 2050. "Our continued use of fossil fuels is pushing us to a point of no return."

GAY MARRIAGE

Says marriage is between a man and woman, but opposed a constitutional ban on gay marriage.

HEALTH CARE

Supports nationalized health care for all Americans and cost controls on medical care.

IMMIGRATION

Supports President Bush's call for a guest worker program that would grant legal status to illegal aliens.

IRAQ

Opposed Iraq war from beginning. Supports "careful" withdrawal of U.S. troops.

TAXES

Wants to raise income taxes and reinstate the "death tax." Says Americans "didn't need" President Bush's tax cuts.

★ ★ ★ ★ ★ ★ ★ ★ ★ ★

5

FRED THOMPSON

Fred Thompson is an unhurried man. He doesn't rush his words, which meander like molasses. He feels no compulsion to race from one event to another. He will get where he's going in his own sweet time.

So it was perhaps not surprising when Thompson became the last major figure to announce his candidacy for the 2008 presidency. The former Tennessee senator, best know for playing District Attorney Arthur Branch in the TV series *Law & Order,* figured there was no sense in rushing such a momentous decision. Besides, he was doing just fine as a noncandidate.

By the summer of 2007, he had passed two declared candidates, Mitt Romney and John McCain, in national polls of Republican White House hopefuls. The only person he trailed was Rudy Giuliani.

"I can't afford to announce," Thompson deadpanned. "I'm doing too well."

But even as a noncandidate, Thompson took pains to remain engaged in the national conversation. In May 2007, for example, he took a swipe at liberal filmmaker Michael Moore for making a documentary, *Sicko,* that portrayed America's health care system as inferior to Cuba's.

"Elements in Hollywood have been infatuated with the Cuban commander for years," Thompson marveled in a column published by *National Review.* "It always leaves me shaking my head when I read about some big-time actor or director going to Cuba and gushing all over Castro. And, regular as rain, they bring up the health care myth when they come home."

As expected, Moore fired back by challenging Thompson to a debate over health care. He even ripped Thompson's well-known fondness for Cuban cigars. But instead of rising to the bait, Thompson responded with a video that he posted on Breitbart TV, a burgeoning website for online video news. The video opened with a large leather chair slowly turning to reveal Thompson removing an unlit cigar from his mouth. Peering over his glasses toward the camera, Thompson addressed himself directly to Moore.

"You know, I've been looking at my schedule, Michael, and I don't think I have time for you," he began with avuncular condescension. "But I may be the least of your problems. You know, the next time you're down in Cuba visiting your buddy Castro, you might ask him about another documentary filmmaker. His name is Nicolas Guillen. He did something Castro didn't like, and they put him in a mental institution for several years, giving him devastating electroshock treatment.

"A mental institution, Michael," Thompson concluded with a pause. "Might be something you ought to think about."

Thompson replaced the cigar in his mouth and slowly turned his chair back to the camera, as if resuming more important tasks.

The thirty-eight-second video was viewed millions of times, proving that Thompson knows how to harness new forms of media in getting his message out. Some conservatives even went so far as to say that Thompson reminded them of another actor who became the Great Communicator as a beloved president—Ronald Reagan.

GROWING UP IN A HURRY

Fred Dalton Thompson was born on August 19, 1942, in Sheffield, Alabama, moving to Lawrenceburg, Tennessee, shortly thereafter with his father, a used-car salesman, and mother, a homemaker. Young Fred grew to be a six-foot-five athlete who excelled on the football and basketball teams at Lawrence County High School. But he was an underachieving student. His girlfriend, Sarah Lindsey, became pregnant while Fred was still sixteen, so the young lovers got married shortly after he turned seventeen. Fred became a father while still attending high school, which forced him to mature in a hurry.

"I was a teenage husband and had three wonderful children early," Thompson recalled.

Despite the demands of his growing family, Thompson managed to graduate from Memphis State University in 1964 with majors in philosophy and political science. Three years later, he received his law degree from Vanderbilt University and returned to his hometown of Lawrenceburg, Tennessee, where he joined his wife's family in a law firm, Lindsey & Thompson.

Two years later, Thompson was named Assistant U.S. Attorney for the Middle District of Tennessee and began prosecuting a string of bank robberies, eventually winning convictions in fourteen of fifteen cases.

Meanwhile, the young prosecutor began dabbling in Republican politics. In 1970, he helped Bill Brock oust three-term Tennessee senator Al Gore Sr. Two years later, Thompson worked on Tennessee senator Howard Baker's successful re-election campaign.

Baker rewarded his protégé by appointing him minority counsel on the Watergate committee in 1973. Thompson moved to Washington and ended up making history by asking what turned out to be a momentous question of Alexander Butterfield, an aide to President Nixon.

"Mr. Butterfield, are you aware of the installation of any listening devices in the Oval Office of the president?" he queried.

"I was aware of listening devices, yes, sir," Butterfield replied, setting off a chain of events that led lawmakers to Nixon's incriminating tape recordings.

As the scandal grew, another young lawyer came to Washington to become a staffer on the House side of the Watergate probe. Her name was Hillary Rodham.

Following Nixon's resignation in 1974, Thompson wrote a book about his Watergate experience, *At That Point in Time,* which was published in 1975. By now he was a lobbyist and lawyer who divided his time between Tennessee and Washington. He took on the case of Marie Ragghianti, who had been fired from the Tennessee Pardons and Paroles Board for refusing to release prisoners who had bribed the administration of Tennessee governor Ray Blanton. The scandal eventually forced Blanton from office and landed Thompson his first role as an actor. That's because the case was made into a movie, *Marie,* in which Thompson played himself. The 1985 film also starred Morgan Freeman, Jeff Daniels, and Sissy Spacek.

Thus began a long string of roles for Thompson in films such as *The Hunt for Red October* and television shows such as *Law & Order.* The six-foot-five actor's stoic demeanor and soothing Tennessee drawl allowed him to project an amiable authoritativeness that suited his roles as presidents, prosecutors, and military officers. Friends said there wasn't a lot of acting involved.

Thompson, who divorced his wife in 1985, discovered that his Hollywood celebrity came in handy in the political world. In 1994, he mounted a campaign for the U.S. Senate seat vacated by Al Gore Jr., who had become vice president two years earlier. Crisscrossing the state in a red pickup truck, Thompson turned on the charm and won the election. Just days after arriving in Washington, he delivered the Republican rebuttal to a speech on taxes by President Bill Clinton. The next day, the *Washington Post* reported that Thompson's "charismatic delivery of the GOP response was reminiscent of Ronald Reagan."

Thompson's star power was not lost on journalist Sam Donaldson, who put the freshly minted senator on the spot by suggesting he was presidential material. Thompson demurred with his trademark down-home humility, which of course only made him seem more presidential.

"There's one thing, I think, for certain that I've observed around here over the period of time that I've been here, and watching all this for years, and that is when people come to town, somewhere along the line, if they do anything at all, if they're shown to be able to put one foot in front of the other, they're mentioned for the national ticket," he marveled. "So now you've mentioned me, and I appreciate it, so we can move on to more serious topics."

Thompson was re-elected in 1996 and spent much of the next year chairing a Senate investigation into Democratic fund-raising abuses. During this period, he dated a variety of beautiful women, including country music singer Lorrie Morgan.

Thompson planned to seek another term in 2002, but reversed course when his thirty-eight-year-old daughter, Elizabeth Panici, died unexpectedly after suffering a heart attack. The tragedy devastated Thompson.

"I simply do not have the heart for another six-year term," he said.

In a rare display of public bitterness, Thompson savaged a Tennessee newspaper that published details of his daughter's death, including her accidental overdose of prescription medicine.

"Every public official has to understand that he or she is a public official and that's the price you pay. For the most part, that's appropriate," he fumed at a press conference. "That's the price your whole family pays. There are lines to be drawn. I think it's extremely unfortunate and uncalled for for the local newspaper to discuss the details of this. Her death obviously played in my decision, but the details of all of that, what news value does that have? Why did she have to pay that price? Why does her little five-year-old boy have to pay that price because her daddy chose to try to serve his state and his country? It's over the line and more like the *National Enquirer*-type stuff than anything else."

Later that year, Thompson married lobbyist Jeri Kehn and joined the cast of *Law & Order*. He started filming episodes even before he officially left the Senate.

Yet Thompson never completely left politics. In 2004, he introduced President Bush at the Republican National Convention. The following year, he agreed to shepherd Supreme Court nominee John Roberts through the confirmation process.

THE REAL CONSERVATIVE?

By 2006, conservatives who were dissatisfied with the GOP field of presidential contenders had begun talking up Thompson as a potential heir to Ronald Reagan's legacy. Thompson was intrigued but decided to see how his rivals performed before getting in himself.

"I'm giving some thought to it," he allowed to Chris Wallace of Fox News in March 2007. "Part of it is internal, a little self-examination on my part. Adlai Stevenson, I guess it was, said, you know, the trick is to do what's necessary to be president and become president and still deserve to be president. And that's serious consideration."

The following month, Thompson returned to Fox and informed host Neil Cavuto that he had a nonaggressive form of lymphoma. He said the cancer was in remission and would not pose a long-term health threat.

"I have had no sickness, no symptoms; I wouldn't know I had it if the doctor hadn't told me that I had it," Thompson said. He added that if the cancer resurfaces, modern medicine "can maintain it, you know, indefinitely, and it shouldn't affect your lifespan at all."

Thompson said it was important to disclose his cancer so that he could gauge public reaction before completing any political plans.

"I'm thinking about running for president. There are certain things you have to check off, in my mind, in order to do that," he said. "You have to decide whether or not, in my case, the man fits the times, and you are needed and you can do something for your country. Those are major considerations."

There were also personal considerations.

"I have got a young family at home, and I'm not going to abandon them," he vowed. "If it turned out that I didn't feel like I could do it without abandoning my family, and, you know, going on the road for months at a time, and for all practical purposes, just checking every once in a while. I wouldn't do that.

"Life is too short for that, under any circumstances," he added. "And I don't think it has to be done that way. I know people will expect that of everyone to run frenetically around for years. And I don't do frenetic very well."

Thompson's reluctance to abandon his family during what would surely be a grueling campaign was interpreted by his critics as further evidence of a "laziness" that he had exhibited during his years in the Senate. He complicated the problem during his interview with Cavuto by making statements that raised the question of whether he had the requisite fire in the belly for the job.

"I have never really craved to be president," Thompson acknowledged. "But I do have a desire to be able to do those things that only a president can do. And that is to have the opportunity to lead your country through perilous times."

Later, when he finally announced his candidacy, he made a point of saying, "I'm going to give this campaign all that I have to give."

That announcement did not come until September 2007, many months after most of the other major White House hopefuls. He sought to present himself as the one true electable conservative. To that end, he stood squarely with President Bush on the war in terror.

"Iraq and Afghanistan are current fronts in this war and the world watches as our will is tested," Thompson said. "Our courage as a people must match that of the brave men and women in uniform fighting for us. We must do everything in our power to achieve success and make sure that they and their families' sacrifices are not made in vain. They know that if we abandon our efforts or appear weak and divided, we will pay a heavy price for it in the future."

During one of his Fox appearances, Thompson made clear he had no use for Democratic carping over Iraq.

"People think that if we hadn't gone down there, things would have been lovely," he marveled. "If Saddam Hussein was still around today, with his sons, looking at Iran developing a nuclear capability, he undoubtedly would have reconstituted his nuclear capability. Things would be worse than what they are today."

At the same time, Thompson acknowledged that the United States blundered in post-Saddam Iraq.

"We've got to rectify the mistakes that we've made. We went in there too light, wrong rules of engagement, wrong strategy, placed too much emphasis on just holding things in place while we built up the Iraqi army, took longer than we figured. Wars are full of mistakes. You rectify things. I think we're doing that now."

Thompson also adopted a tough stance against abortion, although some conservatives doubted his sincerity. That's because the *Los Angeles Times* reported that in 1991, Thompson lobbied on behalf of a pro-choice group, the National Family Planning and Reproductive Health Association. The organization wanted clinics that receive federal money to be allowed to counsel women to have abortions.

"Clearly, I did some work for them," Thompson acknowledged to *National Review* in 2007. "I don't remember what I did, but clearly I did something, so I was representing a pro-choice group."

Thompson also worried conservatives on taxes, immigration, and campaign finance reform, the same issues that had caused John McCain so much trouble with the Republican base. In 2001, Thompson voted for the McCain-Feingold campaign finance reform, which sharply curtailed unlimited "soft" political donations. Conservatives said it also curtailed free speech.

"People could give politicians huge sums of money, which is the soft money situation at that time, and then come before those same politicians and ask them to pass legislation for them," Thompson later explained. "I mean, you get thrown in jail for stuff like that in the real world. And so I always thought that there was some reasonable limitation that ought to be put on that. And you know, looking back on history, Barry Goldwater in his heyday felt the same thing. So that's not a nonconservative position, although I agree that a lot of people have interpreted it that way."

In 2006, Thompson took a moderate stance on illegal immigrants.

"You're going to have to, in some way, work out a deal where they can have some aspirations of citizenship but not make it so easy that it's unfair to the people waiting in line and abiding by the law," he said. "Look, it's just not realistic that we're going to round up 12 million people and ship them all out of the country."

In 2007, when asked by Wallace whether he would raise gasoline taxes to lessen U.S. dependence on foreign oil, Thompson did not answer directly.

"You're getting a little bit further down in the weeds than I want to go right now. I don't know. I'm studying it. I don't know the answer to that question," he said. "We're going to have to do some things differently. We're going to have to think differently about solutions."

He added: "Things have got to be on the table, because we can't keep funding a part of the world that's causing us so much problems."

Later, during his interview with Cavuto, Thompson talked about the need for "sacrifice" in a way that is often considered code for tax hikes.

"There is going to have to be a different way of looking at doing things by the party, and a different attitude, in some respects, by the American people, in terms of responding to a call for sacrifice when it is called for," he said. "I don't think that we have been called on enough."

Although Thompson avoided saying exactly what the taxpayers should be called on to do, he made clear that he would have no compunction about doing the calling.

"I would speak plainly and truthfully to the American people, and if they responded to the message I think the way—if they understood the necessity to do things that need to be done, you would have the support there and you would have a basis for reaching a consensus with Congress."

While Thompson will undoubtedly need to reassure conservatives on taxes, abortion, immigration, and campaign finance reform, he has already won them over on other issues, including Scooter Libby. The former chief of staff to Vice President Cheney was convicted of lying to investigators in the Valerie Plame CIA leak case, even though prosecutors never charged anyone with an underlying crime. Thompson, who aggressively raised money for Libby's defense, was outraged by the verdict and called for a presidential pardon.

"This is a miscarriage of justice," he railed. "It's not fair. And I would do anything that I could to alleviate that."

Thompson also sought to position himself as the only candidate who could defeat Hillary Rodham Clinton.

"To my Republican friends, I point out that in 1992 we were down after a Clinton victory," he recalled. "In 1994 our conservative principles led us to a comeback and majority control of the Congress. Now you don't want to have to come back from another Clinton victory. Our country needs us to win next year, and I am ready to lead that effort."

In the months leading up to Thompson's official entry into the presidential race, he seemed to have difficulty putting together a team to run his campaign. Advisers were hired and fired with a frequency that raised eyebrows in the press. But in the end, Thompson surrounded himself with a seemingly competent team of advisers. It remains to be seen whether they can transform a make-believe president into the real thing. But even if he falls short, Thompson seems prepared to take it all in stride.

"One advantage you have in not having this as a lifelong ambition," he mused, "is that if it turns out that your calculation is wrong, it's not the end of the world."

WHERE FRED THOMPSON STANDS
ON THE ISSUES

ABORTION

Pro-life. Would like to see *Roe v. Wade* overturned.

CLIMATE CHANGE

"Climate change is real, we have to take it seriously," Thompson told voters in New Hampshire. "We don't know what the significance of it is going to be to us."

GAY MARRIAGE

Opposes gay marriage.

HEALTH CARE

Opposes notion that "government bureaucrats can take over our entire medical industry—which, by the way, is the best and most complex in the world—and make it better."

IMMIGRATION

Opposes President Bush's call for a guest worker program that would grant legal status to illegal aliens.

IRAQ

Supports President Bush's policy in Iraq.

TAXES

Supports President Bush's tax cuts.

6

JOHN EDWARDS

John Edwards leaned conspiratorially across the table, as if he did not want anyone else in the bustling North Carolina restaurant to hear what he was about to say. I had just asked him to explain how he might have changed between his presidential campaigns of 2004 and 2008.

"The biggest difference," he confided, "is that then, I spent most of my time thinking about how I could be a better candidate. Now, I spend all my time thinking about how I can be a better president. And it's just a totally different mind-set. It changes everything, having been through it."

The fabulously wealthy trial lawyer whom *People* magazine had once named "sexiest politician alive" was now aspiring to something nobler.

"There's a latent hunger in this country to be inspired

again," he told me. "You look at the presidents that most Americans think of as great presidents and great leaders, and almost to a person they were inspirational. The Democrats would think about John Kennedy; the Republicans would talk about Ronald Reagan. But both had big, inspirational visions about where America needed to go."

Can Edwards join this pantheon of inspirational leaders? Not unless he can get past his reputation as a prettified, silver-tongued ambulance-chaser with a lot more sizzle than steak.

UP BY HIS BOOTSTRAPS

Catharine Juanita "Bobbie" Wade was eighteen when she married nineteen-year-old Wallace Reid Edwards. A year later, they had a son, Johnny Reid Edwards.

"At the time of my birth in Seneca, South Carolina, in 1953, my parents lived in a three-room, white wood-frame cottage in the Utica 'mill village'—a neighborhood where the company owned all the houses and rented them out to the employees in the town's mills," Edwards wrote in his 2004 book, *Four Trials*. "Whenever we relocated—and we did so five times before I was twelve—it was always a move required by the company my dad had worked for since the day he'd graduated from high school in 1951."

His mother worked full-time in a bathing-suit factory. In her spare time, she also sewed "many of my clothes," Edwards recalled.

He and his mom also spent a lot of time playing basketball at a vacant lot near their home.

"I can't begin to count how many afternoons I spent shooting baskets there with my mother (who had been something of a star on her high school team)," he wrote in *Trials*.

Edwards was so influenced by TV shows like *The Fugitive* and *Perry Mason* that at age eleven he wrote an essay entitled "Why I Want to Be a Lawyer."

"Probably the most important reason I want to be a defense attorney is that I would like to protect innocent people from blind justice the best I can," the boy wrote.

Rereading the essay decades later, Edwards was amused by the fact that "to an eleven-year-old, the concept of justice being 'blind' sounded ominous, not one bit virtuous."

During his boyhood, Edwards was blissfully unaware of his family's humble socioeconomic status.

"Back then, a world of greater privilege hardly even registered on my consciousness," he wrote.

As he grew older, he began to spend his summers working in the mills. At age seventeen, his job was to clean hundreds of filthy looms.

"They were slick with grease and lint," Edwards recalled. "And because most of the loom fixers chewed tobacco to pass the time, they were also smeared with rank globs of thick, brown saliva. 'Now you see,' my dad said, bending close to me so that I could hear him over the din of the looms, 'why you need to go to college.' "

Clemson University had been a "missed dream" for his dad, so Edwards resolved to "give him some part of his fantasy" by winning a football scholarship to the storied school.

"I made the freshman team as a walk-on wide receiver at

Clemson," he wrote in *Trials*. "But my slim success as a college player was a far cry from what it had been in high school."

He added: "Since I wasn't big enough to play for a top-level college team, I soon realized that I was unlikely to make varsity and so I was not going to get the athletic scholarship I needed to continue at Clemson. So after only one semester I had to leave the school that meant so much to both me and my family. I wasn't used to failure, and I was miserable that I had failed my dad."

He transferred to the North Carolina State University in Raleigh, determined to work his way through college in three years. He succeeded and, in 1974, graduated with a bachelor's degree in textile technology. But he still wanted to be a lawyer, so he headed to nearby Chapel Hill and enrolled in law school at the University of North Carolina. It was there that he met and fell in love with a fellow student who was nearly four years older, Elizabeth Anania, the daughter of a Navy pilot. After graduating in 1977, John and Elizabeth took the North Carolina bar exam and then got married a few days later in a sweltering country church.

"I had the eleven-dollar wedding ring that I placed on her finger as she placed a twenty-two-dollar ring on mine," he recalled.

The newlyweds had a one-night honeymoon at a hotel in Williamsburg, Virginia. The next day, they headed to Virginia Beach to meet Elizabeth's parents, who would be arriving later in the day.

"Elizabeth and I had no credit cards, and we discovered that between us we could not manage the twenty-two-dollars in cash for the motel room," Edward recalled. "We could only scrape up twenty dollars, and that included change we found on the floor of the car."

So he and his bride spent several hours waiting in the hotel lobby for his in-laws "to arrive and front us an extra two dollars. I have always wondered what they said, or even thought, about their new son-in-law on that night. I have never asked."

RAINMAKER

For the next year, Edwards served as a law clerk to U.S. District Judge Franklin Dupree, a Nixon appointee described by Edwards as "an ardent conservative." In 1978, Edwards began his first job as a licensed attorney at a law firm in Nashville.

"The city never quite felt like home to Elizabeth and me," he later wrote.

So, in 1981, the family, which now included two-year-old Wade, moved back to Raleigh, where Edwards joined another law firm. The following year, Elizabeth gave birth to a daughter, Cate.

Edwards spent the next few years handling run-of-the-mill legal work that failed to excite him.

"I was restless," he recalled. "I pined for a case that could swallow me up."

That case arrived in 1984, when Edwards met a destitute alcoholic who blamed a doctor's prescription for his brain damage. Eventually, the defense offered a settlement of $750,000 and the client instructed Edwards to "take it." Although Edwards had never handled a medical malpractice case before, he wanted to hold out for a bigger payout at trial. His client acqui-esced, remarking, "I trust you," which Edwards later called "the single most terrifying thing anyone had ever communi-cated to me."

That trust turned out to be well placed, as the client won an eye-popping jury award of $3.7 million. Lawyers in such cases typically take a third of the cash.

"I had found my calling," Edwards wrote in *Trials*.

According to Edwards, other attorneys in the area soon began making remarks such as, "Edwards snuck up on 'em. Edwards got lucky. Edwards won because of his hair."

Unfazed, Edwards took on the case of six-year-old Jennifer Campbell, who had been born with brain damage and was di-agnosed with cerebral palsy. Edwards argued that the damage had been caused during childbirth and could have been avoided if the doctor had opted for a caesarean delivery. The lawyer ac-cused the doctor of failing to pay attention to the fetal heart monitor, which would have indicated the baby was in trouble.

"I had to become an overnight expert in fetal monitor read-ings," Edwards later recalled.

Once he mastered this arcane subject, Edwards actually im-personated the unborn Jennifer in front of the jury, pleading during the botched delivery, "I need out." This would raise eyebrows in legal circles for years to come, but Edwards was just getting warmed up. He continued to channel Jennifer as a brain-damaged six-year-old.

"She speaks to you through me," he told the jury. "And I have to tell you right now—I didn't plan to talk about this—right now I feel her, I feel her presence; she's inside me, and she's talking to you. This is her. What I'm saying to you is what Jennifer Campbell has to say to you. And this is what she says to you. She says, 'I don't ask for your pity. What I ask for is your strength. And I don't ask for your sympathy, but I do ask for your courage. I ask you to do what I've done for the last six years. I ask you to be courageous.' "

Edwards added: "I've got a five-year-old boy who is almost the same age as Jennifer, and I can't look at him now without thinking about her."

The performance paid off, winning an award of $6.5 million.

"The jury had returned a record-breaking verdict," Edwards exulted. "Headlines on nearly all newspapers in the eastern part of the state trumpeted the record."

But the judge later ruled the verdict excessive and cut it in half.

"I had never been angrier in my entire life," said Edwards, who refused to accept the reduced verdict.

So a new trial was ordered. After years of additional legal wrangling, the case was settled out of court for $4.25 million. Edwards was now a rich man. He and Elizabeth were raising their children in a lifestyle that would have seemed unimaginable to the son of a mill worker.

"We flew to Europe with them when Wade was eight and Cate was five," Edwards recalled.

In 1993, Edwards and an old friend from law school founded their own law firm, Edwards & Kirby.

"We had often talked about our hopes of starting a small practice that would focus on a very few catastrophic injury and product liability cases, and it was now becoming a reality," he recalled in *Trials*. "Edwards & Kirby did well from the start, and by 1995 our business had doubled."

That summer, he and Wade traveled to Africa and climbed the continent's highest peak, Mount Kilimanjaro. The following winter, the family flew to New York.

"While the girls took in *Beauty and the Beast* on Broadway, Wade and I splurged on scalper's tickets and watched the Knicks play the Kings from some of the best seats in Madison Square Garden," Edwards recalled.

By now, Wade was working at his father's law firm as the "office gofer" and talked of joining the company someday. In February 1996, Wade was chosen as a finalist in an essay contest sponsored by Voice of America. The family traveled to Washington to watch Wade accept the honor.

"We shook hands with First Lady Hillary Clinton and visited the White House," Edwards said.

"THE ACHE OF UNBEARABLE PAIN"

On April 4, 1996, Edwards and his family planned to gather at their beach house on Figure Eight Island in North Carolina. Wade, now sixteen, began driving east on Interstate 40 in his Jeep Grand Cherokee. The rest of the family arranged to join him later. John and Elizabeth were packing at home when the police car drove up.

"There are fierce crosswinds on certain stretches of that interstate, and one of them had swept my boy off the road," Edwards later wrote. "Wade was dead."

The loss devastated Edwards.

"Nothing in my life has ever hit me and stripped everything away like my son's death," he wrote. "It was and is the most important fact of my life."

For weeks, "the ache of unbearable pain" effectively paralyzed Edwards and his wife, he said.

"We felt nothing in that house but Wade's absence, and I can remember little about that time except that Wade was gone," Edwards recalled. "Cate saved us or at least taught us to save ourselves. She pulled two chairs together as a makeshift bed and slept beside us every night. She asked me to keep coaching her soccer team. She made us gifts and made us dinner. The three of us held on to each other."

Edwards, who describes himself as a "devout Christian," did not return to his law office for six months. When he finally did, it was to take on what would become the biggest case of his life.

"A little girl needed my help," he wrote. "And I suppose I needed hers."

The girl was Valerie Lakey, eight, whose intestines had been ripped out three years earlier by the suction from an uncovered drain at the bottom of a wading pool. Valerie survived but was severely handicapped. Edwards now went after the drain manufacturer with a vengeance.

"My work for Valerie Lakey gave me refuge from despair," he wrote. "In those months as I struggled to come alive again, more than life itself I needed to do something strong and good, and I would give it to Valerie—and also in my own private way to my son."

On the day Edwards delivered his closing argument, the courtroom was packed with fellow lawyers who came to hear the man who had become something of a local legend.

"I knew that there was no one who could have beaten me in that courtroom," Edwards later allowed. "When I worked for the Lakeys, I was the best lawyer of my life, and I did the best lawyering of my life."

On January 13, 1997, the jury awarded the Lakeys $25 million, the largest verdict in North Carolina history.

"I WAS WRONG"

In the space of twenty years, Edwards had transformed himself from a law clerk so broke that he had to bum two dollars from his father-in-law to a feared and respected trial lawyer who had amassed tens of millions of dollars in personal wealth. With money no longer a problem, he began to think about public service, reasoning that "if you can't help enough people being a lawyer, consider being a lawmaker."

In 1998, Edwards mounted a successful campaign against Republican senator Lauch Faircloth of North Carolina. The dynamic trial lawyer with boyish good looks made quite a splash in Washington. In 2000, *People* magazine named him "sexiest politician alive." Two years later, Edwards was on Al Gore's short list of potential running mates. Gore ended up picking Connecticut senator Joe Lieberman, who, like Edwards, was considered a political moderate. In fact, Edwards was a member of the New Democrat Coalition, the congressional arm of the Democratic Leadership Council, a group of centrists that included President Bill Clinton.

In 2002, Edwards cosponsored Lieberman's Iraq War resolution and warned on the Senate floor that Saddam Hussein was a truly dangerous dictator.

"Almost no one disagrees with these basic facts: that Saddam Hussein is a tyrant and a menace; that he has weapons of mass destruction and that he is doing everything in his power to get nuclear weapons; that he has supported terrorists; that he is a grave threat to the region, to vital allies like Israel, and to the United States; and that he is thwarting the will of the international community and undermining the United Nations' credibility."

Edwards was among seventy-seven senators in the Democratic-controlled chamber to vote for the resolution, which gave President Bush the authority to wage war on Iraq.

Two years later, Edwards defended his vote even as he tried to unseat Bush from office. The senator had been chosen as Democratic presidential nominee John Kerry's running mate after abandoning his own bid for the White House.

"The vote on the resolution was the right vote, even in hindsight," Edwards told Bloomberg in October 2004. "It was the right vote to give the president the authority to confront Saddam Hussein."

After Kerry lost the presidential contest, Edwards left Washington, since he had not run for re-election to his Senate seat. His wife, Elizabeth, had been diagnosed with breast cancer, but survived the disease.

Over the next several years, Edwards quietly and methodi-
cally began laying the groundwork for a 2008 presidential bid.
He traveled frequently to states with early primary contests.
He built support among Democratic activists and voters before
the field became crowded with better-known candidates such
as Hillary Rodham Clinton. He made real headway, especially
in Iowa, site of the first-in-the-nation caucuses.

"There's a lot of residual goodwill and loyalty from the time
I spent there campaigning for president" in 2004, Edwards
told me.

Edwards returned to Iowa so often during the 2008 cycle
that his oft-used sound bite from the 2004 cycle about being the
"son of a mill worker" became a punch line.

"I go there now and tell jokes about being the son of a mill
worker and everybody laughs. That's because the last time
around, I spent half my time talking about my bio. But now I
don't have to," he told me. "You know why? These people
know me. So instead I talk about what should be happening in
the world, what should be happening at home."

Abandoning his previous persona as a moderate, Edwards
made a conscious decision to move leftward this time around.
Barely a year after defending his support for the Iraq War as
"the right vote, even in hindsight," Edwards reversed course
and declared "I was wrong." The startling admission was
aimed at winning the support of liberal activists and "netroots"
who were exerting an increasing level of influence over the
Democratic Party. Edwards's mea culpa also distinguished him
from Democratic rival Hillary Rodham Clinton, who refused
to apologize for her support for the Iraq War resolution.

Up until early 2007, Edwards seemed to be making headway toward establishing himself as the most credible Democratic alternative to Hillary. But then Illinois senator Barack Obama jumped into the race and instantly relegated Edwards to third-place status. It was a tough blow to someone who had spent years carefully laying the foundation of his campaign.

An even tougher blow came when Elizabeth Edwards, who had given birth to two additional children late in life, learned in 2007 that her cancer had returned. Although it was incurable, she vowed to treat the disease and convinced her husband not to drop out of the race. She became invaluable to his campaign and even launched attacks against rival candidates.

Meanwhile, Edwards made his share of mistakes. He was embarrassed to admit that he had been paying four hundred dollars for his haircuts. This cemented his reputation as a pretty boy, prompting conservatives to renew their taunts of "Breck girl," a reference to an old shampoo advertisement. On YouTube, the wildly popular video-sharing website, someone posted footage of Edwards fussing with his hair for a remarkably long time while the song "I Feel Pretty" played as the soundtrack. Even John Kerry, during the 2004 campaign, had bragged that he and Edwards had "better hair" than Bush and the balding vice president Dick Cheney.

It was also difficult for Edwards to gain much traction with his talk of humble roots, especially after he moved into a 28,200-square-foot mansion, the largest and most expensive house in all of Orange County, North Carolina.

"The recreation building contains a basketball court, a squash court, two stages, a bedroom, kitchen, bathrooms, swimming pool, a four-story tower, and a room designated 'John's Lounge,' " reported the *Carolina Journal* newspaper.

Such opulence made it tough for Edwards to be taken seriously when he tried to discuss the perils of global warming and other environmental issues. Yet he insisted that he remained "the small-town son of Bobbie and Wallace Edwards."

WHERE JOHN EDWARDS STANDS ON THE ISSUES

ABORTION

Pro-choice. Opposes partial-birth abortion except to save the life of the mother.

CLIMATE CHANGE

Wants mandatory cuts in emissions. Has come under fire for asking Americans to conserve energy while he lives in a 28,200-square-foot mansion.

GAY MARRIAGE

Opposes gay marriage, but also opposes a constitutional ban on gay marriage.

HEALTH CARE

Favors universal coverage. "The only way to cover everybody is to mandate it."

IMMIGRATION

Supports President Bush's call for a guest worker program that would grant legal status to illegal aliens.

IRAQ

Voted to authorize Iraq war in 2003, but now says: "I was wrong." Wants most U.S. troops out of Iraq, but some stationed nearby as a rapid-reaction force.

TAXES

Wants to raise taxes on Americans making more than $200,000.

7

JOHN McCAIN

John McCain tries to preempt my questions about his age by bragging about a three-day hike through the Grand Canyon, an anecdote that has the added benefit of demonstrating his spirituality.

"I happen to believe in evolution, but when I stand on the rim of the Grand Canyon, I know that the hand of God was there, somewhere," the Arizona senator told me. "You could not have that beauty without the hand of God being there."

Propping his feet on a coffee table in his Senate office, Mc-Cain downplayed the fact that, if elected, he would be the oldest president ever to take the oath of office. A President McCain would be seventy-two on inauguration day (Ronald Reagan was sixty-nine). Moreover, a two-term McCain presidency would feature an eightieth birthday party nearly five months before he left office. That would make McCain America's first octogenarian-in-chief.

"No, I have no question about it: My health is excellent. I'm still very vigorous. I work eighteen-hour days routinely," said McCain, a skin cancer survivor. "I understand that that could be a concern, just as it was a concern about Ronald Reagan.

"But by showing you one of my weekly or monthly schedules, you would be favorably impressed with at least my activity level," he deadpanned. "If not my good sense."

Such is the self-effacing humor that, when combined with a willingness—nay, *eagerness*—to admit every fault before his detractors can point it out, defines McCain's unique charisma. But while his compulsion to share his shortcomings seemed refreshing back in 2000, when McCain first ran for president, the shtick may be wearing a bit thin in the 2008 cycle.

Still, no one can deny McCain's status as a bona-fide war hero. On four separate occasions, the man strapped himself into warplanes that conked out in midair, sank to the bottom of the sea, blew up before takeoff, or sustained a catastrophic missile strike—all while he was still inside. He also endured considerable torture during a five-and-a-half-year stint in the Hanoi Hilton, which included two years of maddening solitary confinement.

But such heroism may not be enough to compensate for McCain's long history of alienating his fellow Republicans. The congenital contrarian has crossed conservatives on taxes, immigration, campaign finance reform, and a host of other hot-button issues that will not be forgotten anytime soon—certainly not during the 2008 presidential campaign.

As McCain himself acknowledged at the conclusion of his memoirs, "My time might be passing."

DESTINED FOR THE NAVY

John Sidney McCain III grew up idolizing his father, John Sidney McCain II, and grandfather, John Sidney McCain Sr., both of whom were powerful admirals in the Navy. But the military lifestyle prevented the McCain family from staying in one place for very long.

"Our family lived on the move, rooted not in a location, but in the culture of the Navy," McCain recalled in a memoir, *Faith of My Fathers*. "I learned from my mother not just to take the constant disruptions in stride, but to welcome them as elements of an interesting life."

A rebellious child, McCain often found himself in trouble at school.

"When I was disciplined by my teachers, which happened regularly, it was often for fighting," he wrote.

And so, at fifteen, he was sent to a boarding school outside Washington, D.C.

"The Episcopal High School class of 1954 was all male and all white," wrote McCain, recalling the "racial bigotry and gender segregation of the times."

McCain describes himself as a "hell-raiser" in high school, "frequently sneaking off-campus at night to catch a bus for downtown Washington, and the bars and burlesque houses on 9th Street."

As the son and grandson of naval officers who shared his

name, McCain resigned himself to the reality that he would follow in their footsteps by attending the Naval Academy in Annapolis. He described the school as "a place I belonged at but dreaded."

"My father never ordered me to attend the Naval Academy," he noted. "Neither do I recall any arguments with my parents about wanting to consider an alternative future. I remember simply recognizing my eventual enrollment at the Academy as an immutable fact of life, and accepted it without comment."

McCain chafed at the Academy's strict rules and humiliating hazing rituals.

"I hated the place, and, in fairness, the place wasn't all that fond of me, either," he recalled. "I was an arrogant, undisciplined, insolent midshipman. . . . In short, I acted like a jerk."

At night, he and his friends would often blow off steam by prowling the streets of Annapolis.

"Mainly we drank a lot of beer, occasionally we got in fights, and once in a while we found girls willing to give us the time of day," he recalled.

McCain had better luck with the opposite sex during a training voyage that included shore leave in Rio.

"There I met and began a relationship with a Brazilian fashion model, and gloried in the envy of my friends," he recalled.

Returning to the Naval Academy, McCain ended his "four-year course of insubordination and rebellion" by graduating fifth from the bottom of his class. He headed to Florida for flight training and then to Texas for advanced flight training.

"My orders left me enough time to take an extended holiday

in Europe," he wrote, "to meet my new girlfriend, the daughter of a tobacco magnate from Winston-Salem, North Carolina. We were in Paris during the summer of de Gaulle."

While many of his fellow officers were getting married, McCain relished his playboy lifestyle.

"I drove a Corvette, dated a lot, spent all my free hours at bars and beach parties, and generally misused my good health and youth," he recalled.

"I spent my years as a junior officer in the same profligate manner I had spent my Academy years," he acknowledged. "I did not enjoy the reputation of a serious pilot or an up-and-coming junior officer."

Nor did McCain have much luck with airplanes.

"I crashed a plane in Corpus Christi Bay one Saturday morning," he recalled. "The engine quit while I was practicing landings. Knocked unconscious when my plane hit the water, I came to as the plane settled on the bottom of the bay. I barely managed to get the canopy open and swim to the surface."

Such mishaps continued when McCain went to the Mediterranean for several tours in the early 1960s.

"I knocked down some power lines while flying too low over southern Spain," he recalled. "Cut off electricity to a great many Spanish homes and created a small international incident."

McCain's overseas duty was characterized by "long nights of drinking and gambling," he recalled. The lifestyle continued during his next assignment, which entailed working for an admiral in Florida. But he eventually entered into a serious relationship with a former model he had known since his days at the Academy. Carol Shepp, a Philadelphia divorcée with two young boys, had once been engaged to one of McCain's classmates in Annapolis.

"We had been dating for less than a year when I realized I wanted to marry Carol," McCain recalled. "The carefree life of an unattached aviator no longer held the allure for me that it once had."

McCain married Shepp in 1965 and adopted her sons. Soon they had a daughter of their own. McCain's bad luck with airplanes continued, however, as evidenced by an incident on the eastern seaboard in December 1966.

"As I was preparing to come in to refuel, my engine flamed out and I had to eject at 1,000 feet," he recalled.

Nonetheless, McCain was becoming "eager to build my reputation as a combat pilot" and began lobbying to be sent to Vietnam. By 1967, the effort paid off, and McCain found himself on an aircraft carrier, the USS *Forrestal,* in the Gulf of Tonkin, from which he launched bombing runs over North Vietnam. On July 29, he strapped himself into his plane and was getting ready to take off when another plane on the deck accidentally fired a rocket directly at McCain's aircraft.

"A Zuni missile struck the belly fuel tank of my plane, tearing it open, igniting 200 gallons of fuel, and knocking one of my bombs to the deck," McCain recalled in *Faith.* "My plane felt like it had exploded. I looked out at a rolling fireball as the burning fuel spread across the deck. I opened my canopy, raced onto the nose, crawled out onto the refueling probe, and jumped ten feet into the fire. I rolled through a wall of flames as my flight suit caught fire. I put the flames out and ran as fast as I could to the starboard deck."

The thousand-pound bomb that had been knocked from McCain's plane now sat cooking in the flames.

"The bomb exploded, blowing me back at least ten feet and killing a great many men," McCain wrote. "Small pieces of hot shrapnel from the exploded bomb tore into my legs and chest. All around me was mayhem. Planes were burning. More bombs cooked off. Body parts, pieces of the ship, and scraps of planes were dropping onto the deck. Pilots strapped in their seats ejected into the firestorm. Men trapped by flames jumped overboard. More Zuni missiles streaked across the deck. Explosions tore craters in the flight deck, and burning fuel fell through the openings into the hangar bay, spreading the fire below."

The chain reaction caused nine major explosions on the flight deck and countless smaller ones. The disaster killed more than 130 men and injured scores of others. McCain survived, but his misfortunes were just beginning.

CALAMITY JOHN

On October 26, 1967, McCain was on a bombing run over Hanoi, dodging fierce antiaircraft fire from the North Vietnamese. An alarm in the cockpit alerted him that he was being targeted by a surface-to-air missile (SAM).

"At about 3,500 feet, I released my bombs, then pulled back the stick to begin a steep climb to a safer altitude. In the instant before my plane reacted, a SAM blew my right wing off," he recalled. "I radioed, 'I'm hit,' reached up, and pulled the ejection seat handle. I struck part of the airplane, breaking my left arm, my right arm in three places, and my right knee, and I was briefly knocked unconscious by the force of the ejection."

After landing in a lake in the middle of the city, McCain was hauled ashore by angry Vietnamese who broke his shoulder with a rifle butt and stabbed his ankle and groin with a bayonet. He was taken to a nearby prison, nicknamed the "Hanoi Hilton," where he would spent the next five and a half years, including two in solitary confinement. He underwent torture and was denied proper medical treatment of his crash-related injuries, which never healed properly and very nearly killed him. When his captors discovered that McCain was the son of a top admiral, they offered to set him free. But McCain refused to be released before fellow prisoners of war who had been in captivity longer.

Despite his heroics, McCain later reproached himself for occasionally cracking under the pressures of torture.

"I should not have given out information about my ship and squadron, and I regret very much having done so," he wrote. "The information was of no real use to the Vietnamese, but the Code of Conduct for American Prisoners of War orders us to refrain from providing any information beyond our name, rank and serial number."

McCain also was coerced into signing a trumped-up "confession," which also caused him remorse.

"I had failed when I signed my confession, and that failure disturbed my peace of mind," he lamented. "I felt it blemished my record permanently, and even today I find it hard to suppress feelings of remorse."

McCain said he "prayed more often and more fervently than I ever had as a free man." He also learned a great deal from the ordeal.

"My refusal of early release taught me to trust my own judgment," he concluded. "Both my confession and my resistance helped me achieve a balance in my life, a balance between my own individualism and more important things."

After being released from prison and returned to the United States, McCain underwent extensive physical therapy and even regained his flying status for a time. He later became the Navy's liaison to the Senate, which whetted his appetite for a career in politics. One of his duties was to escort congressional delegations on foreign trips, including a journey to China in 1979. During a stopover in Hawaii, McCain, forty-two, met Cindy Hensley, twenty-five, a rich, blonde, beautiful heiress from Arizona who was vacationing with her parents.

"I spotted her at a cocktail reception," he recalled, "and immediately made my way over to her and introduced myself.

"She was lovely, intelligent, and charming, seventeen years my junior," he added. "By the evening's end, I was in love."

He was also still married to Carol, who had been severely injured in a 1969 car crash, while McCain was in Vietnam. McCain, who had not been faithful to his wife since returning to the States in 1973, now spent months dating Cindy while still living with Carol. In his second memoir, *Worth the Fighting For,* he cryptically acknowledged his marital faults.

"My marriage's collapse was attributable to my own selfishness and immaturity more than it was to Vietnam, and I cannot escape blame by pointing a finger at the war," he wrote. "The blame was entirely mine."

McCain divorced his first wife in February 1980 and married his second wife three months later. Knowing by now that he would never match his father and grandfather in attaining the rank of admiral, McCain retired from the Navy and moved with Cindy to Arizona in order to prepare for a congressional run.

"McCain abandoned his wife, who had reared their three children while he was in Vietnamese prisons, and he then began his political career with the resources of his new wife's family," marveled the *New York Times,* noting that Carol nonetheless remained supportive of her ex-husband's career. "He must be the only politician around who could cheat on his wife and divorce her and still get her support."

McCain was elected to the House of Representatives in 1982, thanks in part to one hundred thousand dollars in campaign contributions from businessman Charles Keating and his associates.

"I became friends with Charlie," McCain recalled in *Fighting.* "On several occasions, he invited Cindy and me to his beautiful vacation retreat at Cat Cay in the Bahamas, flying us there, with our infant daughter, Meghan, and her nanny, on his private jet."

"He entertained us lavishly," McCain wrote. "We would all crowd on his yacht, off for a day of swimming and snorkeling, and then return for another extravagant party with the best wine, food, and entertainment available."

He added: "Supporters like Charlie were not easy to come by for a first-time candidate, and I made damn sure that he knew how much I appreciated his support."

But McCain's appreciation went too far in 1987, when he met with federal regulators on behalf of Keating, who was embroiled in a scandal over failed savings and loans. McCain, who had just been elected to the U.S. Senate, later called his intervention on Keating's behalf "the worst mistake of my life." That's because the meetings caused a major scandal for McCain and four other senators, who collectively became known as the "Keating Five." The case dragged on for years, with McCain eventually being reprimanded by the Senate Ethics Committee for his "poor judgment." In spite of the scandal, McCain was re-elected to the Senate in 1992 and 1998.

In 2000, he mounted his first run for the presidency, challenging Texas governor George W. Bush for the Republican nomination. Opting to skip the Iowa's first-in-the-nation caucuses, McCain instead concentrated on New Hampshire's first-in-the-nation primary. He held hundreds of town hall meetings in which he answered questions from voters with a winning mix of candor and self-deprecating humor. He also charmed the press, granting virtually unlimited access to reporters who accompanied him on his campaign bus, the "Straight Talk Express."

"We couldn't buy the TV, we couldn't buy the radio" ads, McCain told me. "There was no way we were going to be able to pay for media, so we had to rely on earned, free media and that was part of our calculation."

The resulting wave of positive press coverage helped

McCain win New Hampshire, throwing a major scare into Bush. But Bush came back to win in South Carolina, leading to McCain's withdrawal from the presidential race. Although some McCain aides bitterly blamed his defeat on a "smear campaign" orchestrated by Bush in South Carolina, McCain disagreed.

"I was defeated in year 2000 by President Bush because he had the party apparatus, the financial base, and he was a better candidate," McCain told me. "That's what beat me."

He added: "There were, of course, people who felt that I was not nearly as appealing to the base as President Bush was."

CONSERVATIVE APOSTASIES

Eight years later, one of the most influential members of the Republican base—Grover Norquist, head of Americans for Tax Reform—called McCain a "traitor" to the conservative cause.

"He's told press people off the record that he would support a tax increase if elected," said Norquist, a charge he repeated on his Tax Reform website.

When I asked McCain whether he indeed had confided to reporters that he would raise taxes, the senator was rendered momentarily speechless.

"And Martians are going to land in Scottsdale tomorrow and pigs fly," he finally sputtered. "I don't know how to respond to something like that. I mean, I have a clear record. I've never voted to raise taxes. Why in the world would I ever tell someone that I would do something which is in direct contradiction to my entire record?"

Yet McCain did vote against several of President Bush's tax cuts, a move he regretted after mounting a second White House bid.

"At the time I was very worried, with some legitimacy, about cutting taxes and not reining in spending," he told me. "I felt very strongly that we were in a war and were going to have to pay for the war.

"The reality is, and I would freely admit, that revenues have increased. And I think that tax cuts have had a major impact. Plus, they've helped the economy."

McCain was similarly penitent about his support for Bush's guest worker proposal, which would grant legal status to illegal immigrants. Many conservatives vehemently oppose consideration of a guest worker program until the U.S.-Mexico border is secured.

"I will freely admit to you that when I first got involved in this issue, I did not give enough emphasis . . . to the concern that people have," he said before spelling out that concern. "We may just have a repeat of the 1980s, where you give amnesty, you don't do enough to seal the borders and then, ten years from now, there's another 10 or 11 or 12 million" illegal immigrants.

He adds: "From numerous town hall meetings, gatherings, et cetera—I am much more aware of this concern."

One area where there is little room for rapprochement between McCain and the conservative base is campaign finance reform. Along with liberal Democratic senator Russ Feingold, McCain cosponsored the McCain-Feingold campaign finance reform bill of 2002, which conservative purists regard as a violation of their rights to political free speech.

"Is there some ill will about campaign finance reform? Yes," McCain told me. "And I understand that it's just a strong difference of opinion."

The same goes for McCain's opposition to a constitutional amendment banning gay marriage, which he concedes has "caused some controversy." Although he opposes gay marriage, McCain believes an amendment should be used only to counter a Supreme Court ruling sanctioning such unions.

If that happened, "I would sign up for a constitutional amendment—like that," he says, snapping his fingers.

McCain also acknowledged "there's still some ill will out there" over his role in the Gang of Fourteen—a bipartisan group of moderate senators that averted a showdown over Bush's judicial nominees in 2005, when Republicans still controlled the Senate. Some conservatives said they would have preferred the fight so that they could strip Democrats, once and for all, of the power to filibuster judges.

Yet McCain's compromise, which limited Democrats to invoking the filibuster only under "extraordinary circumstances," resulted in the swift confirmation of several long-stalled nominees to the lower courts. A more far-reaching effect was the inability of Democrats to block Bush's nominees to the Supreme Court, John Roberts and Samuel Alito.

"I can stand on a record of what we've been able to achieve in getting President Bush's judges to the courts, especially Alito and Roberts," McCain told me. "I think Roberts will stand as one of the great Supreme Court justices in history."

One of the major reasons that conservatives don't like Mc-Cain is that journalists do. Conservatives believe the mainstream media have a liberal bias, so they are naturally suspicious of media darlings like McCain.

Citing McCain's "fan club in the mainstream media," blogger John Hawkins of Right Wing News told me: "There is no Republican up on Capitol Hill more disliked by his own GOP brethren than John McCain."

McCain acknowledges getting a free ride from the press, even as he disputes the widely held conservative conviction that most journalists have a liberal bias.

"One of the reasons that media people spoke favorably of me in the year 2000 was because we gave them access," he told me. "Media people want access so they can write a story. But does that skew their reporting and judgment? I just think they're too professional to do that. They have their reputations at stake."

He added with a shrug: "Most public journalists that I know—I could tick them off: David Broder, David Ignatius, Tom Friedman; you know, the leading news media people in America—I couldn't tell you whether they're Republican or Democrat, liberal or conservative."

Yet the Republican base would never mistake such columnists for conservatives. To them, McCain's failure or unwillingness to grasp these distinctions is yet another reason not to trust him.

Still, even conservatives grudgingly give McCain credit for

remaining steadfast on perhaps the most important issue of all—the aggressive prosecution of the war against terrorism. Although McCain has had his disagreements with Bush over tactics, he supported the overthrow of Iraqi dictator Saddam Hussein and opposes a timetable for the withdrawal of U.S. troops from Iraq.

Conservatives also deeply admire McCain's status as a genuine war hero who was tortured in a Vietnamese prison. Unlike Democratic senator John Kerry, whose relentless focus on Vietnam helped torpedo his own White House bid in 2004, McCain rarely speaks of his Vietnam service without prompting.

As for abortion, the domestic issue of paramount importance to conservatives, McCain told me, "I have a twenty-four-year consistent pro-life record."

When jockeying for the Republican nomination began in earnest in 2006, McCain consistently ranked at or near the top of the field in most public opinion polls. But in 2007, his support began to decline. Journalists blamed the slide on McCain's support for Bush's policy in Iraq. But McCain's Iraq position was no different from that of rival Republican presidential candidates Rudy Giuliani and Mitt Romney, whose standing in the polls was unaffected. Truth be told, conservatives were finally turning their backs on McCain, especially after immigration re-emerged as a prominent issue. Alarmed by this erosion of support, which translated into a major fundraising shortfall, McCain fired his top campaign aides and went back to the shoestring budget that had sustained his renegade White House bid of 2000. But the staff shakeup was viewed by the mainstream media as evidence that McCain could not win the presidency. After championing his cause in 2000, bored reporters now gravitated toward fresher faces in the race, such as Giuliani.

Still, it would be foolish to write off John McCain altogether. He has proven that he performs best in the role of underdog. Who knows? Perhaps even his age will prove no barrier to the presidency. At the very least, he can be forgiven for bragging about his stamina.

"I hiked the Grand Canyon with my son Jack the other day and lost ten pounds while doing it," he reminded me. "We went from rim to rim—Oh God, it almost killed me."

WHERE JOHN McCAIN STANDS
ON THE ISSUES

ABORTION
Pro-life. Would like to see *Roe v. Wade* overturned.

CLIMATE CHANGE
Believes humans are causing global warming. Favors mandatory cuts in emissions.

GAY MARRIAGE
Opposes gay marriage, but also opposes a constitutional ban.

HEALTH CARE
Opposes government-mandated, universal health care.

IMMIGRATION
Supports President Bush's call for a guest worker program that would grant legal status to illegal aliens.

IRAQ
Generally supports President Bush's policy, although he has criticized missteps by the administration. Was an early proponent of a "surge" of extra troops into Iraq to quell violence.

TAXES
Voted against President Bush's tax cuts, but emphasizes: "I've never voted to raise taxes."

8

DARK HORSES

Some people who run for president are actually angling to become vice president. They cannot compete with the top candidates, yet they display enough credibility and likability to sweeten their chances for an eventual spot on the national ticket. Such candidates are effectively employing a back-door strategy for winning the presidency at a later date, since vice presidents often succeed their bosses. This was the career path to the Oval Office for George H. W. Bush and, very nearly, Al Gore. Thus, it is entirely possible that the next vice president will be plucked from the ranks of presidential candidates who fall short of the top prize in 2008. Just don't expect any of these candidates to actually admit their strategy in advance. According to the unwritten rules of selection, the surest way for a veep hopeful to kill his chances is to publicly acknowledge that he is, indeed, seeking the vice presidency.

BILL RICHARDSON

Bill Richardson is a prime example of a candidate who has a better chance of becoming vice president than president. As a popular Hispanic governor with plenty of foreign policy experience, Richardson could provide some balance to a Democratic ticket headed by Hillary Rodham Clinton. Although many pundits expect Hillary to select rival Barack Obama as her running mate, Richardson is arguably a better choice. For starters, he could woo the burgeoning Hispanic vote. Second, his affable demeanor might offset Hillary's somewhat brittle persona. Finally, as a New Mexican, he would bring some geographical diversity to a ticket headed by a New Yorker.

Of course, Hillary would have to carefully weigh these advantages against Richardson's political liabilities. He was tangentially involved in the Monica Lewinsky scandal, having offered Lewinsky a job at the United Nations in what prosecutors called an attempt to buy her silence on behalf of President Bill Clinton. And after leaving his own post at the United Nations to become energy secretary, Richardson was accused by both Democratic and Republican senators of failing to properly safeguard nuclear secrets.

Such controversies have remained dormant throughout much of Richardson's presidential campaign, although they could resurface if he were tapped as Hillary's running mate.

Richardson was born in California, but only because his Mexican mother and Nicaraguan-born father, who had been living in Mexico for twenty years, wanted him to have American citizenship. So they crossed the border into the United States, brought forth the baby, and returned with him to Mexico City, where Richardson said he grew up thinking: "I'm a Mexican and an American trapped in one body." Although bilingual, Richardson "thought and dreamt in Spanish" and "was more comfortable with Spanish," he wrote in his 2005 memoir, *Between Worlds*.

"We enjoyed a comfortable life," he recalled. "We had a chauffeur, Vicente, who would play catch with me when I took up baseball and wanted to practice my pitching. Our cook, Eloisa, treated me like her own son."

Richardson described his father—an international banker who had been raised in Boston—as a "rock-ribbed Republican" who occasionally received phone calls from President Dwight Eisenhower. But Richardson found himself drawn to Democrats.

"I remember the huge press coverage that John F. Kennedy got when he came to Mexico City and he went before the Virgin of Guadalupe and knelt, despite his bad back," Richardson recalled. "He captured all of Mexico by just that gesture, paying tribute to the Mexican matriarch, the Virgin of Guadalupe, going to a church, a very bold, noble gesture. And I was about twelve or so, so I remember that. That had a real impact on me. And Kennedy is my political hero."

In 1961, Richardson moved to Massachusetts to attend high school and college, eventually earning a master's degree from Tufts University. In 1972, he married Barbara Flavin, whom he had met during high school. A decade later he was elected to Congress, where he spent fourteen years representing northern New Mexico. During the mid-1990s, Richardson was dispatched by President Clinton to trouble spots such as North Korea and Iraq. At one point he met directly with Saddam Hussein and helped negotiate the release of two Americans being held captive in Iraq. Clinton rewarded him in 1997 with the ambassador's post at the United Nations, where Richardson quickly got to know the world body's secretary-general.

"Kofi Annan," he recalled, "became a pretty good friend," adding: "We'd also get together socially quite often—with our wives for the movies, without them when we went to the fights."

Richardson said he and his wife were swept up in "New York's social whirl—there is nothing like it anywhere else."

"We got wined, dined and toasted by New York celebrities in the arts, finance, and media, and we entertained at the grand apartment maintained for the ambassador at the Waldorf Towers on Park Avenue," he wrote in *Worlds*. "We had the most fun we ever had."

Less fun was Richardson's entanglement in the Lewinsky scandal. The former White House intern, who had been engaging in sex with the president, now made clear she would go public with the affair if Clinton didn't find her a job in New York. So Clinton instructed his chief of staff, John Podesta, to see if Richardson could find a post for Lewinsky at the United

Nations. Presidential confidant Vernon Jordan later testified that Clinton "was aware that people were trying to get jobs for her, that Podesta was trying to help her, that Bill Richardson was trying to help her."

To that end, Richardson arranged for Lewinsky to come to his Washington apartment at the Watergate at 7:30 A.M. on October 31, 1997. Numerous rules were bent and protocols suspended in order to offer the position to Lewinsky, who ultimately declined. Richardson was later grilled about the unusual episode by prosecutors and a congressional panel. Although some of his answers contradicted the testimony of other witnesses, including some of his own staff, Richardson was never prosecuted.

In 1998, Richardson moved back to Washington to become the energy secretary, a job that caused him additional headaches. In June 2000, for example, he was grilled by members of the Senate Armed Services Committee about security lapses at Los Alamos National Laboratories. Republican senator Richard Shelby of Alabama demanded Richardson's resignation, telling him: "I think it's time for you to go."

Democratic senator Robert Byrd of West Virginia eviscerated Richardson for having delayed his appearance before the committee for several days.

"You've waited and shown contempt of Congress that borders on supreme arrogance," Byrd fumed. "You had a bright and brilliant career, but you will never again receive the support of the U.S. Senate for any office you seek. You have squandered your treasure."

CNN observed that Richardson "looked stunned by the tone taken by many committee members."

Richardson's job at the Energy Department ended when Clinton left office in 2001. The next year, Richardson was elected governor of New Mexico, winning re-election in 2006. That same year, he traveled to Sudan and negotiated the release of an American journalist who had been jailed and accused of espionage. And he began laying the groundwork for a presidential campaign.

But as 2006 gave way to 2007, it became apparent that Richardson would not be a top-tier candidate for the Democratic nomination. He simply was not in the same league as Hillary Rodham Clinton, Barack Obama, or John Edwards. Meanwhile, half a dozen other Democrats were also fighting for a chance at the nomination. And with entire field opposing the Iraq War, it was difficult for Richardson to distinguish himself on foreign policy, which had always been his forte. Although he had long cultivated an image as a moderate, he now decided to run to the left of his better-known Democratic rivals. Since they all favored leaving at least some troops in Iraq (even as they argued for most to be withdrawn) Richardson decided to outdo them.

"I would leave zero troops behind—not a single one," he told a crowd of cheering liberals at the Take Back America conference in Washington in June 2007. "No air bases, no troops in the Green Zone, no embedded soldiers training Iraqi forces."

Conservatives dismissed the statement as shameless pandering. But liberals praised Richardson, whose bold stance had the added benefit of turning up the heat on the more cautious Clinton and Obama.

Will Richardson's gambit be enough to propel him to the presidency? Probably not. But there's always the vice presidency.

WHERE BILL RICHARDSON STANDS ON THE ISSUES

ABORTION

Pro-choice. As president, would apply a pro-choice "litmus test" to his Supreme Court nominees.

CLIMATE CHANGE

Supports mandatory 90 percent emissions cuts by 2050.

GAY MARRIAGE

Voted for the 1996 Defense of Marriage Act, which defined marriage as between a man and a woman. Now says: "I would repeal that horrendous initiative that I voted for and I regret now."

HEALTH CARE

Calls for affordable health care insurance for everyone in America, including illegal immigrants.

IMMIGRATION

Richardson, who was raised in Mexico, wants to grant legal status to illegal aliens. Opposes a border wall as a "terrible symbol between two countries that are friends."

IRAQ

Wants U.S. troops out of Iraq. Unlike Democratic rivals, who would leave some forces in place, Richardson says: "I would leave zero troops behind. Not a single one."

TAXES

Wants to raise taxes by repealing the Bush tax cuts. But promises he will then institute "tax cuts for the middle class."

MIKE HUCKABEE

Former Arkansas governor Mike Huckabee is arguably the best communicator running for president in 2008. He routinely wins the Republican debates and would almost certainly win the White House if the contest were based on persuasiveness or likability. But it is not, so Huckabee automatically tops the short list of vice presidential contenders. He would be particularly valuable if the GOP nominee turns out to be Mitt Romney or Rudy Giuliani. After all, these northeasterners governed the bluest outposts in the nation, Massachusetts and New York City, and have positions on abortion and other social issues that are viewed with extreme skepticism by many conservatives. Who better to balance such a ticket than Huckabee, a Baptist minister from the South with rock-solid conservative credentials on social issues?

Believe it or not, Huckabee was born in Hope, Arkansas, the same small town where Bill Clinton was born nine years earlier. Like a lot of people in Hope, none of Huckabee's ancestors stayed in school long enough to obtain a high-school degree.

"World War I had interrupted my grandfather and World War II had interrupted my father, and before that it just didn't matter because no one who was a male got past the eighth grade because they worked in the fields," Huckabee told me. "And so my heritage was a family that only knew hard work and parents who literally had picked cotton when they were children. And a father whose fireman's job didn't give him enough to really make it, so he had other jobs—building generators on cars. And my mother was a clerk in an office. You know, they worked very hard, but we lived in a rent house until I was in high school."

Huckabee's father was a strict disciplinarian who had no compunction about administering corporal punishment.

"My father was a very patriotic American," Huckabee deadpanned. "He laid on the stripes and I'd see stars."

When Huckabee was thirteen, his family took in a relative who had been stricken with terminal cancer. Young Mike did his part to care for this dying uncle, although by this time the boy was gainfully employed.

"I worked all through junior high, high school, and beyond,

paid my own way through college," he told me. "I got through in just over two years for a four-year degree. Not because I was that much smarter than other people, but because I needed to do it for economic reasons."

Huckabee balanced his heavy class load with a forty-hour-a-week job at a radio station.

"I learned discipline, I learned hard work, I learned that you can't go around whining and complaining about how tough life is," he told me. "You just suck it up and get things done. You know, I consider myself very blessed to have had that experience."

Indeed, it came in handy when Huckabee began his career in communications and eventually founded several religious TV stations, an experience that made him both comfortable and articulate on camera. He also spent a dozen years as a Baptist pastor before deciding to get into politics in the early 1990s.

"I felt there were so many people making decisions in public policy who were sincere and well meaning, but they didn't have a clue as to what the real hurts of humanity were," he told me. "They thought they understood, but they really had never walked into a home where there was no heat. They'd never, ever set down with a family who had just had a complete loss to fire—with no insurance.

"They didn't really know anyone like that. They'd read news stories. But it's a different thing when you literally know those people."

He added: "For every social pathology there is, I can put a name and face to it. It's not abstract to me. If someone talks about a fourteen-year-old girl who is pregnant and hasn't told her parents, I've talked to her."

After a failed bid for the U.S. Senate, Huckabee became lieutenant governor and eventually governor of Arkansas. He also became alarmingly overweight, prompting him to dramatically alter his diet and begin a strenuous exercise regimen. He eventually lost 110 pounds and now runs marathons.

Altough Huckabee is solidly pro-life, he risks alienating a significant segment of the Republican Party with his support for President Bush's controversial guest worker program, which would grant legal status to illegal aliens.

"Yeah, I know, and I think it's one of those things where if people are going to make a decision based on the emotion of that one issue, my attitude is then go ahead and write me off now," he told me. "Because if you don't write me off on this one, you'll find something else later on you're just as mad about."

Take taxes, for example. While Huckabee cut some taxes as governor, he raised others, earning the ire of fiscally conservative groups like the Club for Growth.

"Just because you've cut taxes a couple of times, that doesn't justify raising taxes," said Andrew Roth, the club's director of government affairs. "One of the biggest components of the Republican Party platform is low taxes—and Mike Huckabee does not espouse that view."

Huckabee said he supported Bush's tax cuts and wants to make them permanent. But he also said he wants to further "raise the threshold for paying income tax," which would shift

a greater tax burden onto middle- and upper-income earners—something Bush has been doing for years.

"The Club for Growth for some reason is all on my back
and I think in part because I had the audacity to challenge some
of them—they don't like that," Huckabee told me. "They like
for you to just sort of bow and kiss their ring. And you know,
I'm not going to do that. I don't care who they are."

Huckabee's willingness to cross certain members of his own
party makes him something of a maverick in his own right.

"One of my complaints with Republicans in my own party
is that, true or not, we're perceived as the people whose tax policies do tilt toward the people at the top end of the economic
scale, with disregard to the people who are barely making it.

"And I think it's in many ways a legitimate criticism," he
said. "Certainly we communicate very poorly how our tax policies are going to help the family out there who are barely struggling to pay rent."

Huckabee's years in Arkansas gave him an unusually keen
understanding of the political threat posed to the GOP by Bill
Clinton's wife, Senator Hillary Rodham Clinton, widely regarded as the front-runner for the Democratic presidential
nomination in 2008.

"If the Republicans go around licking their chops, hoping
that Hillary's the nominee because that will be an easy mark,
they're going to be making a huge mistake," he told me. "They
underestimate her at their own peril."

To a lesser degree, some Democrats have quietly said the
same thing about Huckabee, a dark-horse candidate whose
humble roots could blunt any Democratic attempt at class war-

fare. Although he is not yet widely known outside Arkansas, Huckabee has been an inspiration to many overweight Americans with his recent book, *Quit Digging Your Grave with a Knife and Fork*.

In folksy, self-deprecating language, Huckabee tells readers of his lifelong battle with obesity and inspiring journey to healthy living.

"It certainly humanizes me to many people," he told me. "They understand that the struggle they've had—which is the struggle of so many Americans—is something I can honestly relate to."

Huckabee has made obesity a major public policy issue because he believes the attendant health care costs are unsustainable.

"Too many politicians are talking about health care, not enough are talking about health," he told me. "The focus needs to be on health, not health care."

Huckabee devotes so much energy to the health issue that he sometimes sounds as if he's running for surgeon general, not president. This has caused some critics to write him off as a sort of political novelty act.

"They want to ghettoize me as a single-issue candidate, but I'm not," he said. "I would describe myself as a conservative who got there out of conviction, not out of birth, nor out of convenience."

WHERE MIKE HUCKABEE STANDS
ON THE ISSUES

ABORTION

Pro-life. Would like to see *Roe v. Wade* overturned.

CLIMATE CHANGE

Says U.S. should swiftly move away from sources of energy that cause greenhouse gases.

GAY MARRIAGE

As governor of Arkansas, signed legislation banning same-sex marriage.

HEALTH CARE

Preaches exercise and healthful eating to counter obesity and attendant diseases, which he believes are creating unsustainable health care costs.

IMMIGRATION

Supports President Bush's call for a guest worker program that would grant legal status to illegal aliens.

IRAQ

Generally supports President Bush's policy, although he has criticized missteps by the administration.

TAXES

Cut some taxes in Arkansas, while raising others. Wants to make Bush's tax cuts permanent, but also wants to increase the number of lower-income earners who pay no income tax.

ACKNOWLEDGMENTS

My first attempt to profile the 2008 presidential field began way back in the summer of 2006, when I wrote a series of in-depth newspaper articles on the ten most promising candidates of the moment. That series, dubbed *Meet the Next President,* was published in the *Washington Examiner* in September 2006, more than two years before the presidential election (and more than a month before even the midterm elections). This seemed slightly premature to David Yepsen, the legendary political columnist with the *Des Moines Register,* who nonetheless provided me with invaluable guidance.

"Geez, you are off to an early start with these," Yepsen joked. "Makes the rest of us look bad."

Hardly. In the year that followed, four of my ten candidates fizzled. (How was I to know the power of George Allen's "macaca" moment or that John Kerry would make a "botched joke" about supposedly uneducated troops?) Meanwhile, other figures whom I largely ignored emerged as top-tier candidates. Perhaps I was a bit early after all.

On the other hand, six of the people I profiled remained serious candidates. And since many of them granted me lengthy
interviews, it was valuable for me to size them up early, before
they became too guarded and their campaigns became too frenetic. It also gave me a solid foundation of knowledge about
the field, which came in handy when I conducted follow-up
interviews for the book version of *Meet the Next President*.

Others who helped me with the original newspaper series
were Charlie Cook, editor and publisher of the *Cook Political
Report,* and Larry Sabato, director of the University of Virginia's Center for Politics. My coconspirator in hatching the initial
idea was Vivienne Sosnowski, national editorial director of
Clarity Media Group. Her support never wavered as the project grew into a book.

Of course, this book would not be possible without the
boundless enthusiasm of Mary Matalin, head of the Threshold
imprint at Simon & Schuster. I also appreciate the keen editing
eye of Lauren McKenna.

Finally, I owe an enormous debt of gratitude to my wife,
Becky, and our children, Brittany, Brooke, Ben, Billy, and Blair,
for putting up with me while I wrote *Meet the Next President*.

Printed in the United States
By Bookmasters